THE FACTS ABOUT EATING DISORDERS

DID YOU KNOW:

- Eating disorders usually develop during adolescence—a time of intense physical and emotional changes.

- Severe bulimia can lead to gum disease, tooth loss, serious metabolic disorders, and even kidney damage.

- Untreated anorexia nervosa can result in osteoporosis.

- About 6 percent of people with eating disorders will die from starvation, cardiac arrest, or other complications.

- Eating disorders can accompany psychological and psychiatric illnesses such as depression and schizophrenia.

- Excessive weight may not be the health hazard it was once believed to be.

If you're suffering from an eating disorder, now you can do something to help yourself! All the information you need is right here in this insightful and reassuring guide. So turn the page, and begin to learn . . .

WHAT YOU CAN DO ABOUT EATING DISORDERS

What You Can Do About
EATING DISORDERS

Norra Tannenhaus

Foreword by Joel Yager, M.D.

A LYNN SONBERG BOOK

Published by
Dell Publishing
a division of
Bantam Doubleday Dell Publishing Group, Inc.
666 Fifth Avenue
New York, New York 10103

Research about eating disorders is ongoing and subject to interpretation. Although every effort has been made to include the most up-to-date and accurate information in this book, there can be no guarantee that what we know about eating disorders won't change with time. Further, eating disorders sometimes result in symptoms that may be related to other medical or psychiatric problems. The reader should bear in mind that this book should not be used for self-diagnosis or self-treatment; he or she should consult appropriate medical professionals regarding all health issues and before undertaking any major dietary changes.

ISBN: 0-440-21071-2

Published by arrangement with Lynn Sonberg Book Services, 166 East 56 Street, New York, NY 10022

Printed in the United States of America

Published simultaneously in Canada

June 1992

10 9 8 7 6 5 4 3 2 1

RAD

ACKNOWLEDGMENTS

For their patience and generosity with their knowledge and time, the author gratefully acknowledges the assistance of Drs. Joel Yager, Kelly Brownell, C. Wayne Callaway, David Garner, and B. Timothy Walsh in the preparation of this book. Chris Aphis, William Fabrey, and Karen Feinberg also gave invaluable help.

CONTENTS

FOREWORD

Fear of fat pervades our entire society. It seems as if every few months the headlines announce some new product designed to lower calorie intake even more; gimmicky diet books are perennial best sellers; and late-night television advertises an array of machines that are supposed to help you burn more calories than a climb up Mount Everest—without ever leaving your home.

Given this atmosphere, it's not surprising that eating disorders are so prevalent. Eating disorders usually develop during adolescence, a time when young women are struggling with their conceptions of themselves, with physical and emotional changes, and with the new demands of adulthood. Romantic relationships, leaving home, starting families and careers, and establishing one's own life and roots, often in a strange setting, are frightening steps for everybody. Add to this the powerful, if subliminal, message that you're nothing unless you're thin, and you've created a fertile ground for planting the seeds of an eating disorder.

Nevertheless, the question remains, why do some people develop eating disorders while others, coming from virtually identical social backgrounds, do not? The answers seem to involve complex interactions between nature and nurture. Gaining a better understanding of these factors is particularly urgent because these conditions develop early and may last for years, sometimes causing irreparable physical and emotional harm, and even fatalities. Counterbalancing this bleak picture is the fact that treatment proves effective in the vast majority of cases.

This book is valuable because it sheds light on the signs, symptoms, and development of eating disorders. Along with describing some of the warning signs, this book presents some of the psychological characteristics of the people at highest risk for developing an eating disorder, and it presents the most effective methods of treatment currently used. The book also attempts to put in perspective the various contributions that society, family, and the patients' own personalities make to the appearance of these diseases. What's more, it offers practical guidance to people with eating disorders and their families, and a list of organizations to contact for further information and assistance.

Those of us who treat eating disorders have long deplored the "thin-at-any-price" standard of beauty being foisted on society, and how this standard has been promoted to a vulnerable public. At long last, attitudes may be changing as the media, and hence consumers, become more knowledgeable about human biology and nutrition. With its graphic descriptions of eating disorder symptoms and the suffering so many women endure to be thin, *What You Can Do About Eating Disorders* vividly portrays the dangers of pursuing unrealistic ideals. Let's hope the time is near when women are no longer made to believe that body shape determines self-worth.

JOEL YAGER, M.D.
Professor of Psychiatry
University of California, Los Angeles
UCLA Neuropsychiatric Institute

INTRODUCTION

Are you too fat?

If you're like four out of five women in America, your answer to that question will be yes. Eighty percent of adult women want to be thinner, and lots of them are trying to do something about it—according to one estimate, some 80 million people are dieting at any given time.

Americans, American women in particular, want to be slim. We have embraced the ideal of a trim, athletic, slender body, while rejecting the obese image in disgust. We have taken to heart the adage "you can't be too rich or too thin." In such an environment, it's not surprising that eating disorders have reached epidemic proportions. In this country alone, as many as eight million people—the vast majority of them women—suffer from some form of major eating disorder: anorexia nervosa, bulimia, or compulsive eating. These disorders are fueled by a $36 billion diet industry that extols the slender silhouette as the epitome of beauty; by media that take in hundreds of millions of advertising dollars from clothing, cosmetics, and athletic equipment companies; and by movie stars and fashion models whose ubiquitous exposure leads many women to think, "If she looks that way, so should I."

Clearly, however, this isn't the whole story. Everyone is affected to some degree by the surrounding culture, but not everyone develops an eating disorder. Family environment, peer pressure, the role of women in this society, and very likely some inherent personality traits all contribute to someone's risk as well. In fact, those factors are probably just as important as popular culture in contributing to the development of an eating disorder.

There's still lots of controversy surrounding eating disorders: how to treat them, how to prevent them, even how to classify them accurately. But no one disputes their complex nature, nor the frustration virtually all therapists encounter as they try to help people with these problems.

This book is for the person with an eating disorder and those who love her. If you think you know someone who might have such a disease, or if you're afraid you've got an eating disorder yourself, rest assured of two things:

1. You are not alone. As stated above, millions of people share your problem and your despair.

2. Help is available. Treatment methods have advanced tremendously in the 20 or so years since doctors and other health professionals began a serious study of eating disorders. These newer programs are quite effective, and the methods employed, surprisingly simple.

Part I of this book looks at the eating disorders themselves. In the first chapter, you'll learn about the differences between the most common eating disorders. Psychiatrists have developed classification systems that distinguish anorexia from bulimia, although there's a lot of overlap between the two. Compulsive eating remains more of a challenge to diagnose and to treat. Chapter One also introduces you to some of the psychological characteristics of people with different types of eating disorders, a theme that the next few chapters return to in more detail.

Chapter Two concentrates on what is probably the best-known eating disorder, anorexia nervosa. In it you'll discover exactly what the symptoms of anorexia nervosa are, how the seeds of the disorder are sown, and who is at highest risk of developing this disease. In addition, for those who suspect that someone they love has anorexia nervosa, Chapter Two lists some warning signs to look for. Finally, you'll learn about the available treatment options.

Chapter Three covers bulimia, which someone once described as an "ominous variant of anorexia nervosa." Today most experts believe that, despite the overlap between them, anorexia and bulimia are two distinct entities, each with its own unique symptoms and patient populations. The structure of Chapter Three is similar to that of Chapter Two: it covers symptoms, who's most likely to develop bulimia, how the disease begins and develops, the warning signs of bulimia, and the kinds of treatment to consider.

Finally, in Chapter Four, you'll learn about compulsive eating. Compulsive eaters may be male or female, fat or thin, outgoing or shy, gourmets or gourmands—in short, they're a heterogeneous bunch, and it's this heterogeneity that makes this disorder so hard to discover and resolve. Because of its elusive nature and variable characteristics, some researchers doubt whether compulsive eating even belongs in the same discussion with anorexia and bulimia. However, anyone who eats compulsively will tell you that the emotional pain she feels, her frustration and despair, are every bit as real as that experienced by someone with anorexia or bulimia.

Getting the right kind of help at the earliest possible moment is essential for the successful treatment of eating disorders. Part II of this book concentrates on the different modes of therapy currently used in treating eating disorders: psychotherapy, both group and individual; drug therapy; and self-help and support groups.

In Chapter Five, you'll learn how psychotherapy has been used to treat eating disorders. This chapter discusses the pros and cons of group and individual psychotherapy, and which type of eating disorder responds best to which type of therapy. You'll also learn about the strengths and weaknesses of some of the support and self-help groups available, such as Overeaters Anonymous.

Chapter Six looks at the most controversial form of therapy for eating disorders, drug therapy. Research findings about the role of drugs in the treatment of eating disorders are not conclusive, but many doctors feel that drugs are helpful, particularly for patients who may have other problems, such as depression. This chapter describes some of the advantages and disadvantages of drug treatment in general, and goes on to discuss the benefits, limitations, and possible side effects of the drugs most widely used.

Chapter Seven is for the family and friends of someone with an eating disorder. You probably realize that such a disorder takes a serious toll on family life; Chapter Seven offers some advice for those who live with the patient. She's not the only one deserving of help; support groups exist for loved ones as well, and many of the better therapy programs insist that the family get involved. What's most important is to resist the temptation to blame yourself, and to make sure that you have access to help if you need it.

Where to find treatment and support? Chapter Eight lists organizations that can provide you with this information. Many of these groups have lists of doctors, therapists, and programs in a variety of locations; some groups also offer literature, meetings, and hot lines for free or at nominal cost. Even if you hesitate to enter a formal treatment program, there are group meetings you can attend anonymously and for free; there are publications you can read for more information and for the reassurance that you're not alone. For many, that's the first step on the hopeful journey to recovery.

A word about words: Anorexia nervosa and bulimia nervosa are the correct technical terms for those two disorders. When speaking informally, those names are often shortened to "anorexia" and "bulimia." In this book, the double and single-word names will be used interchangeably for purposes of convenience and style. In some circles, bulimia is also called "bulimarexia," which is essentially just another word for bulimia or bulimia nervosa. Some doctors think the term adds unnecessary confusion, and it will not be used in this book.

One of the biggest differences separating anorexia and bulimia is in the sufferer's willingness to seek help. If you're reading this book to learn more about bulimia, chances are you've picked it up out of concern over your own eating habits. Thus, the information on bulimia is directed to you. On the other hand, people with anorexia are notoriously difficult to get into therapy. If you're reading this to learn more about anorexia, it's probably because someone you know has the disease. Therefore, in this book we usually refer to the anorexic as "the patient" or "the sufferer," and speak directly to those of you who care about her.

The vast majority of patients with eating disorders are women, but these diseases also claim a significant number of men. Once again, for purposes of convenience and style, we will usually refer to patients as female, while acknowledging that male patients exist and that their pain is just as real. This book is for them too.

PART I:
THE MAJOR
EATING DISORDERS

CHAPTER ONE

WHAT IS AN
EATING DISORDER?

ANOREXIA NERVOSA: JANE'S STORY

"This started when I was about fifteen, just starting high school," recalls Jane, now twenty. "We had moved to a new town during the summer, leaving behind some really close friends I had known all my life. After we moved, my parents spent most of their time getting settled, trying to adjust, my father to the new job that had brought him to this town, and my mother to the new house and new environment. She also left behind a lot of good friends and a pretty active social life, so she spent a lot of time joining organizations and volunteering for stuff so she could get back into the social whirl. She didn't like having a lot of time on her hands.

"I was never the type to have a lot of friends, but I did have a few best friends that I did a lot with and that I really missed," she continues. "The high school in the town we moved to had a really good football team, and being a member of the cheerleading squad was a really 'in', really social thing for the girls to do. I thought if I joined, I could make some new friends and maybe even help my mother. Maybe she could meet some of the other kids' mothers and become friendly with them." Jane, who has pale skin, big, dark brown eyes, and long brown hair, laughs at the recollection. "Now I realize I was being naive, but at the time I thought that since cheerleading was the 'in' thing for the kids to do, then being friendly with the cheerleaders' parents had to be the 'in' thing for my mother to do. Anyway, to make a long story short, I tried out for the cheerleading squad.

"Anyway, here I was in a new school where I didn't know anybody, living in a new town, my parents off doing their thing. I showed up for the cheerleading tryouts, figuring they'd accept almost anybody who weighed less than two hundred pounds and could follow the routines. I was completely unprepared for what it was really like. It turned out that making cheerleader was really competitive; most of the girls who were interested would spend the entire summer between ninth and tenth grades dieting, getting into shape, sometimes dyeing their hair or even getting nose jobs, for God's sake! The football players hung around and flirted with the girls, you know, teasing them, whistling when they auditioned, stuff like that.

"I was really uncomfortable with all this. I'd always felt self-conscious around boys, and I hated having all these cute, popular guys around seeing me in my gym suit making a fool of myself. Plus, next to some of these girls—some of them were really beautiful—I felt fat, ugly, and clunky. And frankly, I thought they were making fools of themselves, showing off for these boys. I really wanted to just run away, but I was even too self-conscious to do that. I thought I'd just be calling more attention to myself. I figured, just get up, do your thing, go home, and don't ever show yourself on this football field again."

Jane chuckles at the memory, then grows serious. She looks down as she remembers what happened next. "I got up when they called my name and went to the middle of this little part of the field where everyone was standing. The gym teacher who oversaw the cheerleaders started asking me some questions, but while I was talking to her—can you imagine, I heard this even while having a conversation with someone—some guy yelled out, 'thunder thighs!' " At this, Jane takes a long pause, clearly fighting back tears. Finally, composed once again, she resumes her story.

"To tell you the truth, I don't really remember what happened after that. Somehow I got through the tryout and was finally able to leave the field. Needless to say, I didn't make the team. All I remember is that I felt alone, unhappy, inadequate, humiliated, and like I was the fattest pig in the world. I remember telling myself, 'You must really be huge if somebody noticed your thighs that much.' I decided that instant to go on a serious diet and become really thin." Sighing, she fixes her companion with those huge eyes and says, "That's how it started."

The "it" that Jane is referring to was a "diet" that lasted three years and ended only when Jane, weighing 70 pounds (she's 5 feet 4 inches) and shivering from cold even in 90-degree weather, was told by her doctor that if she did not enter a hospital on her own, he would have her committed against her will as a last-ditch effort at saving her life.

BULIMIA NERVOSA: SANDY'S STORY

"I've been bingeing and vomiting for years, at least since college," recalls Sandy, who's now 30. "I was always a big eater, and I always had something of a weight problem, but before I left home I usually managed to keep it under control. I'd exercise a lot, and sometimes I'd go on a really strict diet for a while, then I'd go back to what I called eating 'normally'—which for me could be a whole loaf of bread in one sitting, a pint of ice cream, two or three bags of potato chips. There were certain kinds of food that, once I started eating them, I just couldn't seem to stop. So I'd try to stay away from them as long as I could, until finally I'd break down and go wild.

"But things changed for me when I started college. I had been a straight A student in high school, something I was really proud of. Then I went East to this Ivy League school, and *all* the kids had been straight A students in high school. So I wasn't a star anymore. Not only that, but the work at college was hard. High school was easy for me—I managed to get good grades while having lots of friends, even boy-friends—but in college, I had to struggle to get the kind of grades I was accustomed to, and sometimes I didn't get those grades. I wasn't prepared for it.

"And then of course there was the food. They say college food is bad, but as it happened, I was at a school where the food was pretty good." Sandy laughs, covering her mouth. "I guess I've always known where to go for good food. And on top of that, my school had an ice cream fund. That's right, about twenty years ago one of the alumni, this little old lady, decided that all the students should be able to have ice cream whenever they wanted it, so she actually gave the school a grant to buy ice cream! It was a bulimic's dream—or nightmare, depending on how you looked at it. And of course, on top of all that, there were vending machines in the dorm, and an all-night grocery store just about a block from campus.

"There was just no way I could resist all of that," explains Sandy, whose 5 feet 6 inch, 130-pound figure gives no hint of her struggle with food. "When I look back on it now, I think, maybe if I hadn't found the schoolwork so hard, if I hadn't been so homesick, if I hadn't felt like just one of the crowd, with nothing special to make me stand out . . .

who knows? But then I tell myself that there had to be other factors at work, because everyone else was going through pretty much the same thing, and I knew only a few other people who did what I did."

What Sandy did was to eat more and more, in episodes that became increasingly frequent as her feelings of stress grew. "My pattern of bingeing and vomiting began when I went to the campus coffee shop with a friend of mine one night. We were taking a class together and had been studying for our midterm exam, which we knew was going to be really hard. To make it worse, we were both really behind in our work for that class. So we were feeling really nervous, really scared.

"Anyway, we studied together for a couple of hours, and then decided to get something at this coffee shop on campus before it closed. We'd already eaten dinner.

"When I sat down and read the menu, I started feeling really hungry. *Everything* on that menu looked good—I could have eaten my way through the whole stupid thing. I said to my friend, 'You know, I feel really hungry. I'm going to get a cheeseburger, some french fries, and a chocolate shake. And an order of onion rings.' Francine giggled and said, 'That sounds good. I'm gonna get the same thing.' So we ordered two of everything.

"Well, we felt like partners in crime. We kept giggling and saying, I can't believe I'm doing this—I'm going to have to starve tomorrow—I feel so full, I'm getting sick—but we kept on eating. It turned into kind of a game. When we finished, and believe me we finished it, Francine looked at me and said, 'Let's go whole hog. Let's order a pizza.' Well, I just started laughing, but then I said, 'Sure. Let's do it.' I can't speak for her, but I knew what was happening to me— I knew I was eating like that because I felt stressed-out." Sandy, who had been laughing at her memories a moment ago, now turns very serious. "I remember the feeling exactly," she says, "although it's hard to put it into words. It seems stupid to me now, but at the time I thought there was something colorful, almost romantic about doing something self-destructive because I was unhappy. You know, like all those writers and actors who become alcoholics. When I agreed to have that pizza, I remember thinking to myself, 'What the hell. You only live once. Be outrageous.' So I was.

"Well, after the pizza, we ordered hot fudge sundaes. And by the time we finished those, the place was closing. As we stood up from our chairs, Francine and I looked at each other. We didn't say a word, but we burst out laughing. We walked out of the coffee shop, and began walking in the direction of the all-night grocery store. We'd read each other's minds.

"It would take me another couple of hours to tell you everything we ate that night," Sandy says with a wry smile, covering her mouth again. "We took the food back to her room, and when we ran out of that, we headed for the vending machines. We ate until dawn.

"I'd never felt so sick in my life. I felt like I was pregnant, carrying a hundred-pound baby in my stomach, which wasn't too far from the truth. I also felt oily, dirty, as though all the grease from the food was oozing out through my pores. But at the same time—I know how crazy all of this sounds—there was something reassuring about the way my stomach ached. I focused all my attention on how full I was, how bad I felt, and it took me away from worrying about that exam.

"I said to Francine, 'God, I feel sick. I'm going to starve myself for a week. I bet I've gained twenty pounds tonight.' And she said, 'You don't have to. If you bring all this food up now, before it's all digested, your body won't absorb most of those calories.'

"I couldn't believe what I was hearing. How could I not gain weight after eating at least five thousand calories? You see, I was pretty naive—I had no idea what Francine was talking about. She had to spell it out for me. 'Look, I've done this before. I take a toothbrush or something and stick it down my throat, and throw up all this food. I know it seems pretty gross, but at least that way I can eat and not get fat. I think it'll also help you feel better.' I thought about that. Frankly, I was feeling so sick that the thought of bringing up some of that food did sound like a relief. And if I could eat like that and still not get fat—I decided I'd give it a shot.

"Well, by the time I finished and went back to my room, I just had time for a quick shower before my first class. I felt so ashamed, so embarrassed—the whole incident just seemed so disgusting, not to mention all the money I'd spent on the food—I tried to avoid speaking to anybody for the rest of the day. I just wanted to get back to my room and hide. I tried not to think about it. The next day I felt a little better, and by the following day I was almost able to find some humor in the whole thing. In fact, I was starting to remember the whole experience as kind of fun. And I started thinking about all that food, that hot fudge sundae, the cheeseburger . . . but then I thought, if you do that again you're going to turn into a blimp, even if you vomit your guts out. In fact, I was sure I'd gained weight from the first binge. So I weighed myself, figuring that would help keep me in line. Imagine my surprise when the scale showed me two pounds *lighter* than before the binge.

"I felt like I'd discovered the greatest secret in the world. Here was a way I could eat all that stuff I'd always tried so hard to resist, as much as I wanted, and still not gain weight. I immediately started thinking about what I'd eat that night. I couldn't wait for the day to end. I went to the cafeteria first and had a salad, and impressed everyone with how 'good' I was being. After dinner I went straight to that little grocery store. I rationalized it by telling myself, 'You've been working so hard, it's okay to indulge yourself right now.' I figured I'd bring the food back to my dorm room and eat it while I was studying.

"Well, to make a long story short, I began to live for the binges," Sandy recalls with a sigh. "It didn't happen overnight, of course. I got through that exam week bingeing and vomiting once or twice more, but boy, did I look forward to those binges. And by some miracle I managed to do fairly decently academically, too, although at the time I was mad at myself for not maintaining the straight A average I'd had in high school. After exams, the pressure lightened up a little, and the bingeing and purging kind of receded into the background. I went back to my usual pattern of pigging out —nothing like those binges, of course—and then dieting or exercising or both. But having done the binge-purge thing once, it was easier for me to turn to it again the next time I was under stress, and each time I'd do it more often and the episodes would last longer, until I was bingeing and purging at least once a day, every day, regardless of what was happening in my life. I'd wake up in the morning and immediately start thinking about what I was going to eat."

After two years of therapy, Sandy still struggles with the temptation to binge and vomit. She does give in occasionally, but not nearly as often as she used to. Nevertheless, she carries a legacy of those painful years. When asked why she always covers her mouth when she laughs or smiles, she smiles openly, revealing mottled teeth, eroded from years of contact with the stomach acid she'd vomited up.

COMPULSIVE EATING: MARGIE'S STORY

"I think there's still a part of me that believes that any problem can be made a little better with a banana split," says

Margie, a plump woman of 35. "I've been chubby all my life. I've tried every diet you can name—fasting, liquid protein, kelp-lecithin-vinegar, Scarsdale, Beverly Hills—the list goes on and on. And actually, I'm pretty good at losing weight. I've lost forty or fifty pounds in just a few months on some of these. The problem is, I always gain it all back, and then some.

"I come from a fat family," she admits. "I was a fat kid and a fat teenager. The other kids in school used to tease me all the time about being fat. I hated it. I was miserable. When I was younger, I'd think about starting a diet, maybe even stay on one for a day or two, but then I'd get a craving for some forbidden food, and my willpower would go right out the window.

"I know people say now that obesity may be genetic. That might be partly true in my case, because both my parents are fat. But I think in my case there's more to it. When I was a senior in high school, I developed a crush on my art teacher—in fact, most of the girls in my class had a crush on him, because he was young and hip and really cute. And there were some really pretty girls who used to hang around him all the time, trying to get his attention. He was a nice man and tried not to play favorites, but whose ego wouldn't be flattered by all that? I felt like the fat, ugly kid in the class, and was too shy to ever talk to him, even though I would have loved for him to notice me.

"Anyway, one day I was really down on myself for something—I don't even remember what it was, I was just in a bad mood for some reason. Art class was my last class that particular day, and I remember walking home thinking about how nice Mr. Barrett was and how stupid I was for having a crush on him. I came home—no one else was there. I headed for the kitchen, as usual, and pulled a pint of ice cream out of the freezer. As I piled it into a plate, I thought, 'Go ahead. Make yourself really huge. Then Mr. Barrett will never look at you.'

"Well, I knew instantly what I was doing. I was using food, or my weight anyway, as a way of hiding—I wasn't sure why, or from what, but obviously by eating compulsively and getting fat, I didn't have to get out there and compete against all those other girls.

"I was thunderstruck. I put my spoon down and thought about this insight I'd just had. And then,"—here Margie laughs—"I picked up the spoon again and started eating. Whatever brilliant insight I might have had, it sure didn't stop me from stuffing my face.

"I guess I just love to eat," Margie admits. "I'm not even sure when I'm hungry anymore. I look at the clock, and if it says six o'clock I say, 'Well, time for dinner.' I think about food all the time. If I know there's ice cream or cookies or candy in the fridge, I can't get them out of my mind until I finish them. If something great happens to me, like getting engaged or promoted at work, I go home and eat in celebration. If something terrible happens, like getting fired or divorced, I eat in consolation. The only way I seem to be able to stay away from fattening food is to go on a really strict diet and give up the good stuff completely. Even then, I can't stop thinking about candy, sweets, chocolate. If anything, I think about that stuff more when I *don't* have it than when I *do*. And, like I said, I can stay on the diet for a while, but then I go back to eating my usual way, and I gain back all the weight. So I go through all that for nothing, but I keep trying. I hate myself the way I am. I want to be thin." She giggles, but her eyes look sad. "You see? I feel funny talking about all this, and I can't wait to go home and eat."

Margie was right when she said that obesity was genetic. In fact, people get fat for many reasons, of which overeating is only one. Yet it's her despair over her weight and the attempts she's made to slim down that are at the root of her problems with food.

WHAT IS AN EATING DISORDER?

It's clear that Jane, Sandy, and Margie all have an eating disorder, characterized by an inappropriate relationship with food, or a gross distortion of eating behavior. But eating disorders have repercussions that reach far beyond eating behavior alone. They affect the patient's physical health and emotional well-being, and they impair her social and professional functioning as well—in short, no aspect of a normal life goes unscathed when an eating disorder develops. Sandy, for example, ultimately dropped out of college because she became so obsessed with her binges. Jane became so tired and weak that she stopped participating in any activities that didn't have to do with school or losing weight. And Margie hates her job, but won't look for a new one because she's afraid she'll be rejected due to her size. Other people may be affected in more or less serious ways depending on the severity of their disorders. But is there a woman in America past the age of ten who hasn't had an occasion ruined, even if only for an instant, when she thought, "I don't look good enough. I'm too fat. That woman over there looks better"? Indeed, it's characteristic for these patients to harbor unrealistic expectations of their ideal weight or their ability to maintain it. Does this mean that *every* woman who feels a twinge of self-doubt if she feels fat, or who would like to be thinner than she is, has an eating disorder? Of course not, but these feelings are so widespread that it does give you some inkling as to why eating disorders can flourish.

What's also clear about Jane, Sandy, and Margie is that

each woman is different, and each has a different eating disorder. The following chapters will explore in detail the differences between the major eating disorders. But there are also some important features that the different eating disorders share.

Features Common to the Major Eating Disorders

1. Extreme preoccupation with appearance, body image, or body size. "I always had to be the best-looking woman in the room," Sandy recalls. "Whatever I did, my looks always came first. Of course, it finally got to the point where I'd start planning my next binge as soon as I got up in the morning, then factor in how long it would take me to throw it all up so I wouldn't get fat." That's characteristic of the second feature:

2. Exaggerated fear of getting fat. "At my worst, I'd only allow myself two leaves of lettuce with one teaspoon of ketchup for lunch," Jane recalls. "I'd measure it all out very carefully. God forbid if a little ketchup overflowed the spoon. I was convinced that I'd gain back all my weight overnight. If I thought I'd somehow eaten too much despite my best efforts, I'd exercise an extra hour that day."

3. Exaggeration of body size, body flaws. "Sometimes, as I'm coming out of the shower, I'll see myself in the mirror and just hate myself," Margie admits. "I'll think, 'You fat slob. You're huge.' All I see is a big fat belly, a big rear end, huge thighs, cellulite everywhere."

4. Increasing rigidity of thought and withdrawal from normal activities. Eating disorders can persist for years. The earlier they begin, and the longer they last, the more isolated the sufferer becomes as she withdraws into her own little world of rituals and obsessions she develops around food. In the most severe cases, the sufferer may fill her days with nothing but thoughts and plans about food—the next meal, the next binge, the next bout of exercise. Ultimately, she may derive her entire identity from the eating disorder, feeling special and unique only because she's able to go for so long without eating, or to binge but remain thin because she vomits. In these cases a therapist must help the patient enhance other facets of her personality and develop a stronger identity from those, to weaken the stranglehold the eating disorder has on her life.

INCIDENCE OF EATING DISORDERS

According to estimates from the National Institute of Mental Health, eating disorders afflict 710,000 to 1,420,000 people. However, other estimates run much higher than that; as stated in the introduction, some experts believe as many as 8 million Americans suffer from eating disorders, especially if you take compulsive eating into account as well. Bulimics are thought to outnumber anorexics by about 2 to 1. Recent surveys indicate that the incidence of anorexia nervosa ranges from 1 in 100 to 1 in 800 girls aged 12 to 18, while in a study of college freshmen, 4.5 percent of the women and 0.4 percent of the men met the diagnostic criteria for bulimia nervosa. In all, 1 in every 10 adolescents is thought to be at risk of an eating disorder. Affluent white women and girls compose 80 to 95 percent of the patient population, but doctors are now seeing a growing number of black and Hispanic patients from less wealthy segments of society.

Among people with eating disorders, about 5 percent—

that's 1 in every 20 patients—will eventually recover sponta-
neously, without any treatment at all. Unfortunately, about 6
percent will die, from starvation, or from cardiac arrest or
other physiological complications of eating disorders. On a
more optimistic note, current methods of treatment help
the vast majority of patients.

Eating Disorders in Men

Because women compose the vast majority of people who
develop eating disorders, it's easy to fall into the habit of
referring to patients as "she" or "her." In fact, however, 5 to
20 percent of eating disorder patients are men. According to
the knowledge currently available, men who develop eating
disorders tend to do so at an earlier age than women, but
there is often a history of eating disorders in the family, as
is found in women who develop these diseases. Probably
the most important difference is the background of men
with eating disorders: they tend to come from blue collar or
working-class families, while women with eating disorders
usually come from wealthier backgrounds.

LESS COMMON EATING DISORDERS

In this book, the term "eating disorders" refers to anorexia,
bulimia, and compulsive eating. In fact, however, there are
other types of eating disorders, most of which are extremely rare.

Nonspecific Eating Disorders

These are eating disorders in which someone clearly has a disturbed relationship with food, but the official diagnostic criteria for anorexia or bulimia (discussed in Chapters Two and Three) are not met. For example, a woman who maintains normal weight and does not binge, but sometimes vomits anyway from an irrational fear of becoming fat, could be said to have a nonspecific eating disorder. Similarly, people who have most of the diagnostic criteria for bulimia but binge less frequently, or who meet the diagnosis of anorexia except that they still menstruate, are considered to be suffering from nonspecific eating disorders.

Eating Disorders Associated With Other Problems

Eating disorders may also accompany other psychological or psychiatric disorders such as depression, schizophrenia, or obsessive-compulsive disorder. A change in weight is, in fact, one of the diagnostic features of depression, because some patients become so depressed they simply don't want to eat. On the other hand, it's also not unusual to encounter patients who overeat due to depression and gain weight. Schizophrenic patients may develop bizarre eating habits that reflect the general distortion of reality that characterizes schizophrenia. For example, a paranoid schizophrenic may become too afraid to eat if he thinks people are trying to poison him. And people with obsessive-compulsive disorders may neglect to eat because they are too busy repeating all sorts of rituals that serve to keep distressing thoughts at bay. What sets these patients apart from the ones under study in this book is that they lack the exaggerated fear of fat characteristic of people with anorexia or bulimia or, to a lesser degree, those who compulsively overeat.

Pica

People with the rare but bizarre eating disorder known as pica persistently consume substances that are not nutritious and may even be dangerous, such as paint, string, insects, or even animal feces. Little is known about the treatment or development of pica, except that it occurs most often in children.

CONCLUSION

You've probably guessed by now that people with eating disorders have some important features in common: a poor sense of identity, overemphasis on appearance and pleasing others, and an exaggerated fear of getting fat. Just as important, however, are the differences between each disorder—differences that will be explored in the next three chapters. Remember, however, that while anorexia and bulimia are two separate disorders, there's some overlap between them. Indeed, it's not unusual for someone to have both eating disorders simultaneously, or to develop first one and then another. Or perhaps the person you're worried about doesn't fall neatly into any one category: maybe she starves herself, but binges and vomits occasionally too. Or she may not vomit after a binge, but exercises to the point of exhaustion for the next few days.

What all of this means is that each patient is unique, despite the elements she shares with others who have an eating disorder. As you'll see, recovery involves teaching each patient to love herself *because* she's special and unique, and not because she's thin.

CHAPTER TWO

ANOREXIA NERVOSA

THE WARNING SIGNS
OF ANOREXIA NERVOSA

You probably already know what the most characteristic feature of anorexia nervosa is: self-starvation, due to an irrational fear of becoming fat. In fact, if you're reading this, chances are it's because you suspect that someone you know—a sister, a daughter, a close friend—may be developing anorexia nervosa. Maybe you've even tried to talk to her about it, only to be rebuffed with an answer like, "There's nothing wrong," "I like the way I look," or perhaps, "Mind your own business." In fact, after starvation, denial is perhaps one of the most significant features of anorexia; people with this disease really don't think there's anything wrong with them. They not only resist other people's efforts to help, they resent the interference. Their resistance may be so persuasive that you start thinking, "Am I overreacting to this? Maybe she really is okay—perhaps it's just a phase she's going through." These thoughts are certainly far more comforting than watching someone you love starve herself, but beware! Eating disorders are much more difficult to treat the longer they're left alone. If you're unsure of your suspicions, look for some of these warning signs:

Your friend eats as though she's on a diet, even though she's already very thin. If it seems as if she's constantly watching portions or calories, skipping meals, or just cutting her food into little pieces and pushing it around on the plate, or exercising too much, while already appearing several pounds underweight, she may be on the road to anorexia. Vomiting after meals or abusing laxatives or diuretics are other danger signals, although these are of course harder to confirm. But if she fits the description in other ways *and* frequently runs to the bathroom immediately after eating, be suspicious.

She usually wears clothes that are baggy or too big. One reason why anorexia often persists for years is that the patients become adept at hiding their condition. One of the ways they do this is by wearing clothes that conceal the body. Often, friends or family members don't realize how thin the patient has become until they happen to see her in her underwear or a leotard, when the emaciation is apparent.

She is preoccupied with weight, dieting, shape, and exaggerates the importance these factors play in her life. It's a rite of passage in the United States for adolescent girls to worry about their looks and their weight, to spend hours experimenting with makeup and clothes, and to try different diet and exercise routines. What *isn't* normal is for this to become the central focus of someone's life. If your friend consistently gives up trips to the movies or the mall because she has to exercise, or never wants to eat out anymore because she's afraid it's all too fattening, beware. Remember, however, that this is all a matter of degree; it's one thing to pass on a trip to McDonald's for a short period of time because you're on a diet; it's another to reject your entire social life from an irrational desire to be thin.

She undergoes changes in personality. Many therapists admit quite freely that women with anorexia can be very difficult to like. Secretive, mistrustful, uncooperative, they guard their eating rituals jealously and put off anyone who tries to help them. These features don't develop overnight; they're usually characteristic of anorexia that's pretty well established. Nevertheless, if someone you know well starts becoming more isolated and withdrawn over a period of several months, or seems sad, angry, and irritable, *and* she fits some of the other criteria described above, she may be developing anorexia nervosa.

She experiences dizziness, blacking out, fainting, difficulty concentrating. These are all symptoms of incipient starvation.

DIAGNOSING ANOREXIA NERVOSA

To guide physicians in making the diagnosis, the American Psychiatric Association has established the following as the diagnostic criteria for anorexia nervosa:

1. Refusal to maintain body weight over a minimal normal weight for age and height, e.g., weight loss leading to maintenance of body weight 15 percent below that expected; or failure to gain as much weight as expected during a period of growth, leading to body weight 15 percent below that expected. Thus, if a woman's normal weight is 130 pounds, she would be 15 percent below that at about 110 pounds.

2. Intense fear of gaining weight or becoming fat, even if underweight.

3. Distorted perception of her body weight, size, or shape; e.g., she claims to "feel fat" even when emaciated, or believes that one part of her body is "too fat," even when she's clearly underweight. Jane, at 5 feet 4 inches and 75 pounds, used to stare at herself in the mirror and wail that her stomach was too fat.

4. In women, the absence of at least three consecutive menstrual cycles when otherwise expected to occur.

Thanks to these criteria, diagnosing anorexia nervosa should be a relatively easy job. Doctors know that someone who has all the symptoms described above unquestionably has anorexia nervosa and should be treated as such. But how do you always know if all of these symptoms exist? An anorexic may lie, for example, about the frequency of her menstrual periods. Because of this, you might want to keep in mind some other features that point to anorexia:

• The lack of any other physical or psychiatric disorder that could account for the weight loss or refusal to eat.

• Onset of the disease before age 25. There are cases of anorexia nervosa that have developed in women older than 25. The vast majority of women, however, develop the illness as teenagers. Jane, mentioned in Chapter One, was 15 when she became anorexic.

• The presence of at least two physiological symptoms associated with anorexia nervosa. These symptoms are described in the next section.

• Abuse of over-the-counter laxatives, diuretics, or diet pills. Women with anorexia nervosa often resort to one or more of these products in their zeal to lose weight. It's not unusual for an anorexic to take up to 40 laxatives a day, and in a few extreme cases, patients have admitted taking 300 laxatives *in one day*. Symptoms of laxative abuse include colicky abdominal pain, anal soreness, and fecal incontinence (inability to control one's bowel movements). On the other hand, prolonged laxative abuse may ultimately lead to dependence on them, because the patient discovers she can't move her bowels without using the laxatives.

• Exercising excessively. Women with anorexia may exercise up to five or six hours a day—swimming, running, dancing—the more strenuous, the better. One of the challenges confronting people who treat anorexic patients in hospitals is to prevent them from exercising in secret.

• Osteoporosis. Anorexics run a higher risk of losing bone mass, a condition known as osteoporosis. Osteoporosis makes the bones brittle and more vulnerable to fractures, and in the elderly can lead to severe hip fractures and spinal deterioration. Doctors believe there are several reasons why osteoporosis develops in anorexics: diminished levels of the hormone estrogen, important for the maintenance of healthy bones; increased levels of another hormone, cortisol, which have also been found in anorexic women; and lower intakes of calcium, vitamin D, and protein, as a result of self-starvation.

In general, then, you can be fairly certain that your friend has anorexia nervosa if you observe the following three constant, essential warning signs:

1. Abnormally low body weight.

2. Deliberate maintenance of that body weight through dieting, exercising, abuse of laxatives or diuretics, or a combination of the three.

3. Physical symptoms of starvation.

Symptoms of Starvation

When people don't eat enough to maintain a healthy weight, whether deliberately or due to circumstances beyond their control, they develop certain classical physical and psychological symptoms. The psychological symptoms of starvation influence the treatment of anorexia nervosa and will be discussed later in this chapter. The physical symptoms of starvation include:

• Cold skin, sometimes with a bluish tinge. Called hypothermia, this condition results in part from the loss of so much body fat, which acts as an insulator, that the patient feels cold all the time, even during the summer.

• Pain upon sitting down, because the patient has lost so much body fat that there's no more natural padding over the bones.

• The development of baby-fine hair all over the body, a condition known as lanugo. No one knows why lanugo occurs, but it is common among anorexics and is sometimes accompanied by the loss of hair on the head.

• Hypotension, or abnormally low blood pressure, probably due to a weakening of the heart's activity.

• A weakened heart and the hormonal changes associated with anorexia also lead to an abnormally slow heartbeat, or bradycardia.

• Constipation severe enough to cause abdominal pain. Sometimes a patient doesn't connect the pain and constipation with the fact that she's not eating enough, so she visits a doctor who may then be able to determine the real reason for her discomfort.

• Problems with swallowing, possibly because starvation induces malfunction of the gastrointestinal tract.

• Indigestion following the little food that she does consume, again due possibly to impaired gastrointestinal function.

• Edema, or abnormal water retention. One of the functions protein serves in the body is to maintain normal water balance within the blood vessels, so when someone is starving or deficient in protein, some of that water may escape into tissue, creating a bloated appearance. Edema is relatively common in starving people, but some experts believe that it does not occur among anorexics as often as might be expected.

• Feeling weak or tired, probably because the body simply isn't receiving enough fuel.

• Anemia from insufficient iron and protein intake.

• Lowered metabolic rate, an adaptive response to starvation that allows the body to minimize its fuel needs as much as possible.

• Sleep problems, most likely due to hunger as well as other factors that have not yet been identified.

• Hormonal abnormalities. The most obvious signal of this is loss of menstrual periods, a condition known as amenorrhea. Women usually require 18 to 22 percent body fat for normal menstrual functioning (the average is about 25 percent); below that, menstruation stops. That's why amenorrhea is common among female athletes and ballet dancers (as are eating disorders), as well as women who are starving. A decreased level of estrogen, one of the hormones that regulates reproductive function, is also thought to be one of the factors contributing to the higher incidence of osteoporosis in all these groups of women. What's interesting about anorexics, however, is that some patients experience amenorrhea *before* they lose a significant amount of weight, raising questions about the role of hormonal disturbances in causing the disease.

Psychological Characteristics of Anorexia Nervosa

Along with the physical consequences of starvation, anorexia nervosa has some typical psychological characteristics. You may have read that most anorexics have a distorted body image—that is, they see themselves as too fat regardless of how skinny they become. Indeed, preoccupation with appearance, body size, and reports of feeling fat, or believing that parts of the body are too fat, are hallmarks of the disease. However, experts are now starting to believe that not everyone with anorexia (or bulimia) overestimates her body size. Some studies indicate that these patients see themselves accurately, but are convinced that that appearance is still unacceptably fat. The difference is subtle, but important: the patients' perceptions may be accurate, but their feelings or beliefs about those perceptions are inappropriate. These findings have led many experts to revise their opinions on the psychological components of anorexia nervosa and the proper approach to treatment. More and more, they are coming to realize that one of the most important characteristics of anorexia is not, as previously thought, the patient's inaccurate view of herself, but rather an irrational fear of becoming fat, and a determination to maintain a morbidly low body weight no matter what the cost.

If you live with an anorexic, you may think her behavior seems odd, even bizarre. In fact, however, these activities are not that unusual among people experiencing starvation. In her attempts to control every calorie she ingests and expends, she may avoid eating with others, preferring instead to eat by herself, often at odd hours and in a ritualistic way. And although she's obsessed with being thin and terrified of being fat, the anorexic is simultaneously preoccupied with food, eating, and cooking. She may discuss it to the exclusion of everything else; she may pore over cookbooks and cooking magazines; she may even do all the family's shopping and cooking—then refuse to partake of anything herself. In fact, the word "anorexia" is Greek for loss of appetite, but the truth is that anorexic patients are ravenous.

Why, then, do they persist in their behavior? Accounts from former patients now on the road to recovery may provide the best clue. "It seems sick now, but back then, the more weight I lost, the better I felt," Jane recalls. "I'd allow myself maybe an apple and three crackers for lunch; then I'd raise the ante on myself—see if I could get by with the apple and just two crackers, or just the apple and nothing else. The less I ate, the more special and powerful I felt. Oh, I felt hungry all right, although I would have died before admitting it—I almost *did* die before admitting it," she adds with a wry smile. "But that hungry, empty feeling was how I measured my success. If I went to bed hungry every night, I knew I was being good." Jane's feelings typify those of many anorexics, who derive gratification from losing weight and refusing food despite feeling hungry.

There's more to it, of course. Today most experts agree that anorexia often arises at some turning point in the patient's life. In Jane's case, it coincided with moving to a new town and beginning high school; for other patients, the trigger might be the first menstrual period or, in older patients, getting married or having a child. In all these instances, the crucial event signals the young woman's impending adulthood and the independence society expects her to achieve. As she gets thinner and weaker, the anorexic requires more attention from those around her, and no longer has to worry about going out on her own.

Equally important, anorexia nervosa represents a young woman's cry for attention and, ironically, more control over her own life. This disease typically occurs in girls who have been good students and model children, never giving their parents any trouble. Often, the parents have made the child's most important decisions for her, and she may not have learned how to express her own wishes or needs. Thus, the attention focused on her during arguments over eating and food, and her parents' worries over her strange behavior, may be the most attention the sufferer has received in a long time, and her unusual approach to food may be the only form of control she's able to exert over any aspect of her life.

A clinical psychologist might say, then, that anorexia nervosa fulfills several conflicting needs in the patient: it relieves her of some of the stress of entering adulthood and attaining independence, while simultaneously attracting attention from her parents and offering a measure of control over her own existence.

Binger vs. Restrictor Anorexics

Textbooks give information and provide examples, but as we've emphasized, few people in real life present symptoms exactly as described in books. This is especially true with eating disorders.

Some people with anorexia nervosa lose weight through

diet and exercise alone, usually helped along with laxatives, diet pills, and/or diuretics. Because food restriction is the hallmark of their disease, these patients are called "restrictor" anorexics.

Other anorexics, however, display some of the features of bulimia nervosa as well, i.e., they go through episodes of bingeing and vomiting. These are the "binger" anorexics. Most anorexics in this category binge and purge at least once a week.

Some experts believe that the development of a bingeing pattern marks a deterioration in an anorexic woman's course: she has now gone from excessive control over her eating and exercise to complete loss of control. While other authorities may argue that point, some important differences do distinguish binger from restrictor anorexics:

• Bingers are more likely to have been sexually active prior to the onset of their disease, and they're more likely to remain sexually active while they have the eating disorder.

• Restrictor anorexics have usually developed the disease earlier in life, and tend to be shyer, more rigid and withdrawn than their bingeing sisters. Usually they have not been sexually active and they may even be afraid of sexual relationships.

WHO DEVELOPS ANOREXIA NERVOSA?

Family Characteristics

It would be easy to say, "people develop anorexia because their parents didn't raise them properly." It would be easy, but it would be wrong. Eating disorders arise from the interaction of many different factors, of which family pressures may be just one. And keep in mind the fact that many people with eating disorders come from terrific families— warm, loving, and supportive. Nevertheless, if you are the parent of someone with anorexia, you've undoubtedly bombarded yourself with questions and self-accusations. But the fact is, you didn't create your daughter's eating disorder any more than you can will her to get well. Self-blame is not only misguided, it's counterproductive, because it only makes you feel worse about yourself and your situation.

On the other hand, psychologists have discovered that certain family characteristics *are* typical of women who develop anorexia. They've studied these characteristics, not in an effort to place blame, but to learn more about who's at highest risk of developing eating disorders, and how to help families overcome some of their problems so that every member functions more happily. These characteristics include:

Investment of food, eating, weight, and appearance with great emotional importance. For example, it's not unusual to find patients with anorexia nervosa whose parents or siblings work in the food industry or own restaurants. One woman married the man who managed her father's restaurant.

A family history of anorexia nervosa. Women who develop anorexia often have mothers or sisters struggling with the same problem, which helps confirm the notion that food is a family issue.

Mood disorders in close relatives. It's been found that anorexic patients often come from families in which a first-degree relative—that is, a parent or sibling—has some other emotional disorder such as depression or manic depression. These disorders also frequently accompany anorexia nervosa.

Greater-than-normal stress on appearance and achievement by one or both parents. It's not unusual to discover that the seeds of anorexia were sown when the patient began dieting to please a parent.

Restricted expression of feelings, especially negative feelings. Once in therapy, an anorexic patient often reveals that her family discouraged most spontaneous expression of feelings, but disliked negative feelings such as anger most of all.

An excessively close relationship with parents. There is some evidence that anorexic patients are abnormally dependent upon their parents. You may think this contradicts what was said above, but in fact the two circumstances can be compatible. Many anorexic patients try to fulfill as completely as possible their *parents'* wishes, needs, and expectations, and in so doing fail to express their own desires.

Excessive control by parents over the patient's life. One famous psychiatrist said that some parents "deprive [the child] of the right to live her own life." In other words, they make all her decisions and run her life for her, without giving her a chance to develop an identity of her own.

Failure to acknowledge the girl as an individual in her own right. Many patients report that their parents had high expectations of them, which the patients somehow failed to meet. From all of this comes a picture of a family that gives the impression that it values the girl mainly for what she can do for the family—i.e., enhance its prestige through some achievement such as getting good grades—rather than for who she is as an individual.

Other family problems. Anorexia nervosa often develops in a family atmosphere of tension, fighting, and possibly other problems as well, such as alcoholism or some form of abuse. Many therapists believe, in fact, that the eating disorder may in part be the child's subconscious attempt to "save" her parents, because if they focus on her they don't have to focus on their own problems.

Patient Characteristics

Just as experts have clarified certain family traits that allow anorexia nervosa to develop, they've discovered characteristic traits in the patients. Once again, this has not been done as an attempt to blame the victim, but rather to help determine who runs the greatest risk of developing anorexia nervosa, in the hopes of preventing the problem. Some of these traits include:

A history of being slightly overweight. It's been estimated that about 33 percent of patients were mildly overweight prior to the onset of anorexia nervosa. In fact, the disease frequently begins when the patient starts dieting much as anyone else would, but doesn't stop when she reaches her target weight. Alternatively, she may have lost weight for some other reason, such as an illness, likes herself that way, and decides to continue losing.

An excessive desire to please others and avoid stressful situations. Perhaps because they've learned to suppress their own desires, people who develop anorexia often exhibit an extreme need to conform and to try to make others happy, sometimes at the expense of their own happiness or needs.

A rigid personality, expressed as an excessive need to follow rules and a tendency to be judgmental of others. Much has been written about the rigidity of anorexics; it's thought that such a trait develops from the future patient's need to maintain as much control as possible over her environment, partly because she has so little actual control over her life, and partly because her circumstances may actually be out of control in some way.

Fear of new situations. Women who become anorexic often turn out to have been shy, withdrawn youngsters who avoid new situations. This probably fits in with the issues they struggle with concerning identity and control.

Choice of hobby or career that places great emphasis on weight. Ballet dancing, modeling, acting, and sports careers are all notorious for fostering eating disorders in women, due to the premium placed on looking thin and, ironically enough, "healthy."

Again we should make it clear that all of these problems are intertwined. Eating disorders result from spending a lifetime in a particular social and family environment. What's more, family members are almost always unaware of the impact their behavior is having on the future patient; they'd most likely be shocked if someone were to tell them, "If you never allow your child to make her own decisions, you may be setting her up for future unhappiness." What's also clear is that there are probably other factors at work, factors that doctors have yet to identify, because many people come from situations such as these but do not become anorexic. Thus, blaming the family entirely for one member's eating disorder is as unrealistic as laying the entire blame on society—the real issues are far more complex than that.

THE COURSE OF ANOREXIA

What happens if you decide to take a "wait-and-see" attitude
—perhaps it's just a phase she'll outgrow? Normally, someone who's had anorexia nervosa for several months or years
and doesn't receive treatment eventually stabilizes at about
20 to 30 percent below average body weight. According to
some experts, most patients who receive therapy only experience one episode of anorexia in their lives, and ultimately
return to normal weight. Other investigators dispute those
claims, however, saying that patients must be followed for at
least 4 to 5 years, preferably more, to determine how well
they really do. In studies where patients have been followed
this long after receiving treatment, up to one-third remained
ill: their amenorrhea persisted, and their body weight
stayed low. As mentioned before, people with the most severe cases of anorexia nervosa may quite literally starve
themselves to death; mortality estimates run from 6 percent
to as high as 18 percent—that's nearly 1 in every 5 patients.
According to some evidence, women may die of causes related to anorexia as long as 24 years following treatment—
meaning, of course, that the issues that led to the disease to
begin with were never satisfactorily resolved. One factor
influencing the success of treatment is the presence of
other diseases, such as depression, or bulimia in a patient
who is also anorexic. Then it's up to an astute doctor or
therapist to ferret out all of a patient's intertwining problems, and see to it that she gets help for them.

TREATMENT CHALLENGES

The different forms of treatment—individual psychotherapy, family therapy, drugs, and hospitalization—will be cov-

ered in more detail in Part II. But if you've read this far, it will probably come as no surprise to learn that treating the anorexic can pose quite a challenge. These patients are smart and determined; they've figured out all sorts of ingenious ways to reject calories, and what's more, they don't see themselves as sick. Most anorexics resist help as zealously as they pursue their calorie counts and exercise. Adding to this is the fact that usually an anorexic is still young enough to be living at home, where her behavior affects the entire family. The chances are that if she's going to go for treatment, you or some other "significant other" will have to be the one to get her there, because she won't go on her own. One way to surmount that wall of resistance is to perform an intervention, which Chapter Five describes in detail.

But there's one treatment challenge that's unique to anorexia, and which must be met first if other efforts are to have any success. As one renowned expert put it bluntly, "One cannot do meaningful therapeutic work with a patient who is starving." Starvation, self-imposed or not, distorts one's thought processes and can cause profound changes in personality. This has been documented many times, perhaps most dramatically by a group of scientists conducting research during the second World War.

The Minnesota Experiment

As news of the horrors of World War II started reaching the United States, scientists began to realize that they'd soon be faced with the task of treating thousands, perhaps millions of people who'd been exposed to malnutrition. A group of researchers at the University of Minnesota, led by Dr. Ancel Keys, decided to study the processes of starvation and rehabilitation in detail. This study, which ran from November

1944 through October 1945, became known as the Minnesota Experiment.

The experimenters recruited 32 men, aged 25–26, as subjects for study, which consisted of 12 weeks of preliminary observation, 6 months of semi-starvation, and 12 weeks of rehabilitation. For these robust young men, who normally consumed some 3500 calories each day, "semi-starvation" meant a daily intake of 1500–1600 calories—more than most commercial reducing diets allow today. People in concentration camps received at most about 1000 calories per day. The men's average weight loss was roughly 35 pounds by the experiment's end. The book that resulted from their service and the dedication of Dr. Keys and his colleagues, called *The Biology of Human Starvation,* presents a detailed account of the changes that occur in the human body and mind as a result of slow, prolonged malnutrition.

Prominent among these were effects on the personality. As the researchers wrote, "It was apparent during the second month of semi-starvation that emotional and personality changes were developing in the subjects which . . . might, if they progressed far enough, require expert psychiatric treatment." The men complained of weakness, hunger, sore muscles, and fatigue; they also became increasingly moody, apathetic, and depressed as the experiment continued. Their eating habits also changed; the men "ate silently and deliberately and gave total attention to the food and its consumption. As the starvation progressed, the number of men who toyed with their food increased." Some Minnesota subjects came to linger for two hours over a meal they would normally consume in a few minutes; the experimenters recalled reports of starving prisoners of war who, despite extreme hunger, hoarded their food rations to eat at some later time. The subjects also became preoccupied with food, menus, and recipes, and some even decided to pursue food-related careers after the experiment was over. After a while, the observers noticed that "the men became reluctant to plan activities, to make decisions, and to participate in group activities." Spending time with others became too tiring, too much trouble.

The Psychology of Starvation

The Minnesota Experiment, and others that followed, showed beyond doubt that some psychological changes are characteristic of starvation. Most of these changes abate when the starvation is relieved, but some remain—albeit in more moderate form—for years, perhaps throughout the person's life. Many of the traits seen in anorexia—suspicion, hostility, irritability, isolation, rigid thinking, the development of food rituals, preoccupation with food and cooking—result from the biological changes that accompany starvation. Thus, any therapy for a severely malnourished anorexic is almost certainly doomed to fail unless a balanced nutritional status is restored first. Until then, the mental changes induced by starvation will make it virtually impossible for a therapist to reach the patient on any meaningful level. For most people, there seems to be a critical weight necessary for normal mental function.

Other Aspects of Treatment

The main reason why it's so important to seek professional help is that a severely emaciated anorexic usually requires hospitalization. In the hospital, specially trained doctors, nurses, and therapists can help her get her weight up to a point where she is mentally capable and physically strong enough to be treated as an outpatient. You may have heard horror stories about anorexics being tied down and force-fed; the truth is that anorexics who absolutely refuse to eat, or whose physical condition is especially desperate, may require nourishment through a tube inserted into a blood vessel, but this practice is not as common as it used to be. Instead, the experts around her assure the anorexic that she will receive a healthful diet, in portions that will permit gradual weight gain but won't make her fat. Patient, compassionate, but firm, these professionals have achieved surprising success in getting anorexic patients to eat.

Once the patient has attained a stable weight, she's able to benefit from psychotherapy. Another reason why anorexia is so difficult to treat is that it usually starts when the patient is relatively young, and may persist for years until she gets help. For example, a young woman who becomes anorexic at age 15 and has it until she's 20 will have had the disease for fully 25 percent of her entire life. By then, it's become an important part of her identity, and she may feel lost when trying to function in a world that requires her to eat normally. What's more, remember that many young women develop anorexia because they feel they have no control over their own lives. Also, they may feel reinforced when, at least in the beginning, people say, "You look so thin!" The eating disorder gives them a feeling of achievement, which may be threatened by the prospect of gaining weight. The idea of becoming an ordinary person, with nothing special to set her apart, may be terrifying. Thus, one of the goals of therapy is to allow the person to discover and enjoy the different talents and characteristics that make her a unique human being.

Along with individual therapy, most experts recommend family therapy where anorexia is involved. Parents and siblings may initially deny that any problem exists outside of the eating disorder, but if the sessions are effective, relatives will ultimately come to face the problems that have affected the family's function and contributed to the development of the anorexia. Perhaps one or both parents suffer from depression or substance abuse; maybe the marriage is in trouble or another family member is struggling with an eating disorder. Needless to say, any of these can influence family dynamics in very profound ways. You'll find more on individual and family therapy in Chapter Five.

Drug Therapy

Almost every psychiatric drug on the market has been tried in the treatment of anorexia, without much success. Drug therapy *has* been effective in patients whose anorexia is accompanied by other disorders, such as depression. In those cases, administration of antidepressant medication may ease the depression and make the patient more receptive to therapy for her eating disorder. For more details on the drugs used in the treatment of eating disorders, please see Chapter Six.

CONCLUSION

If you're like most people who live with someone with anorexia nervosa, you've probably wondered, "How did it start? Should I have noticed it earlier? How could I have stopped it?" But how can anyone identify the turning point at which a simple diet becomes a life-threatening disease? Anorexia nervosa is insidious. The more entrenched the disease, the more the patient sheds the vestiges of normal living and becomes a slave to her obsession. Not only that, but those around her become so accustomed to living with her that way, that they may accept the situation as normal.

Many anorexics don't come for help until a doctor or family member finally sees how emaciated the patient really is and insists that she be treated.

Fortunately for many anorexics, their physical condition becomes so extreme that the disease can no longer be denied. Bulimics are often not so lucky, as you'll discover in Chapter Three.

BULIMIA NERVOSA

THE WARNING SIGNS
OF BULIMIA NERVOSA

Perhaps you're pretty certain that the person you're worried about isn't anorexic. She's not emaciated, she appears to eat normally, and yet . . . there's something not quite right. Maybe she spends long hours in the bathroom, especially after meals. Maybe she constantly evaluates herself in the mirror. Maybe she's always running to the supermarket, or she's always broke but doesn't seem to have anything to show for it.

Or perhaps it's your own behavior that's troubling you. You ruminate constantly about the next meal, the next binge, that half-pound you gained this morning. Maybe you find that one bite of a "forbidden" food sends you out of control, until several hours or a few thousand calories later, you drag yourself into the bathroom in disgust. At what point does someone cross the line from an occasional pig-out to a full-blown eating disorder?

As you might have guessed, this is a hard question to answer. One person might think there's something wrong if she binges and purges once a week, while someone else might not realize she has a problem until she eats and vomits several times a day. As with anorexia nervosa, only a doctor can make the diagnosis for sure, but experts at the National Institute of Mental Health (NIMH) suggest the following as warning signs of bulimia nervosa:

Regular binges. This may be difficult to detect in someone else, because bulimics become so good at hiding their behavior. Nevertheless, if someone you care about seems to be eating more than usual on a regular basis, or if there's a chaotic, out-of-control quality about the way she's eating, be alert. If it's yourself you're worried about, bingeing once a week or more is considered a sign of a possible eating disorder.

Regular purges. It's also unlikely that you'd be able to actually observe someone in this behavior, but clues include disappearing into the bathroom for long periods after meals, or the sudden heavy use of over-the-counter laxatives or diuretics. Following your binges with episodes of vomiting or intense exercise is another sign of possible bulimia nervosa.

Weight gain or maintenance, despite frequent dieting and exercising. Someone who always seems to be counting calories when you're with her, but never seems to lose weight, may be secretly bingeing. On the other hand, someone who appears to eat well, yet exercises a lot and seems a bit thin, may be vomiting up her food, exercising too much, or fasting when you're not around—perhaps all three.

Stealing, or abuse of alcohol or drugs. These actions don't guarantee that someone is bulimic, but they are common among people with this eating disorder.

Frequent depression. Again, depression is no guarantee that someone has bulimia, but it often accompanies this illness. Depression in someone who meets the other criteria mentioned here may well be a signal of current or developing bulimia.

Swelling of the cheeks or glands in the neck. Frequent or prolonged vomiting often causes the salivary glands in these areas to swell.

Scars or ulcers on the back of her hands. These again are a giveaway that the individual is possibly forcing herself to vomit by shoving a hand or a few fingers down her throat. Contact with stomach acid or abrasion from teeth may cause the wounds.

DIAGNOSING BULIMIA NERVOSA

By now, you may have formed the impression that bulimia is a complex and baffling disorder. Yet experts believe that twice as many people struggle with it as are struggling with anorexia.

Bulimia is easy to conceal because bulimic patients come in all shapes and sizes. There are anorexic bulimics who do indeed appear emaciated, and there are obese bulimics whose size reflects their struggle with food. And there are many bulimics whose appearance gives no clue whatever of the conflict within.

In general, bulimics tend to be older and more independent of their families than are anorexics. Thus, they've had more time to develop personalities that don't focus completely on the eating disorder. This is a promising feature because it means that a bulimic is more likely to be troubled by her behavior, and to seek and accept help. Usually, her biggest obstacle is her own shame. That's why it's so important to remember that, if you're bulimic, you're not alone.

Indeed, you'll see in the following pages that bingeing and purging are common, even among people who might not meet all the criteria for a diagnosis of bulimia.

What are these criteria? The American Psychiatric Association lists the following:

1. Recurrent episodes of binge eating.

2. A feeling of lack of control over eating behavior during the eating binges.

3. The regular use of self-induced vomiting, laxatives or diuretics, strict dieting or fasting, or vigorous exercise in order to prevent weight gain. You may know someone who binges regularly but doesn't vomit, so you haven't considered her truly bulimic. But although the binge-vomit pattern gets the most attention because of its sensational nature, in fact not all bulimics vomit regularly. Regular binges plus the use of other methods in an attempt to keep weight down can qualify someone for a diagnosis of bulimia. (For the purposes of convenience, in this book we'll refer to any attempt to avoid weight gain after a binge as purging.)

4. A minimum of two binge eating episodes a week for at least three months.

5. Persistent overconcern with body shape and weight. Do you find you can't pass a mirror without at least a quick check? Is your day ruined if you gain a pound? Bulimics obsess continually about their looks, and work hard at being as attractive as possible.

Most doctors believe that anyone who meets these criteria should be considered bulimic. But they also realize that many other symptoms accompany this disease. Some other prominent characteristics of bulimia include:

1. A history of frequent dieting. Many studies have revealed that virtually everyone who develops bulimia has a history of frequent attempts at controlling her weight. In one British study of 32 people with bulimia (30 women, 2 men), every subject described previous attempts at dieting. Even bulimics who appear overweight might be heavier than they are if they didn't exercise tight control over their eating. It's possible that such constant vigilance places the bulimic in such a precarious balance that a stressful event may tip her over into an episode of bingeing. For a fuller explanation of this idea, please see the upcoming section on Restrained vs. Unrestrained Eaters.

2. Symptoms of depression. These include gloomy or pessimistic thoughts; recurrent ideas of suicide; impaired concentration; or increased irritability. It's not uncommon for a bulimic patient to be diagnosed with clinical depression as well as the eating disorder. Some bulimics have a history of attempted suicide.

3. Excessive fear of becoming fat. In one recent study, 92 percent of bulimic patients questioned said they were extremely or very much afraid of becoming fat. Indeed, that's why they purge after they binge—most bulimics believe this is the well-kept secret of weight control that permits them to eat what they want and not get fat. This fear of fat would also be in keeping with the strenuous dieting practiced by so many bulimics or bulimics-to-be.

4. Eating food secretly, or as inconspicuously as possible. Recalls one bulimic, "In graduate school, I lived with two roommates in the same apartment for three years. I think I ate maybe five meals with them in that whole time. They used to tease me and say, 'Jessica, when do you eat? How do you stay alive?' Little did they know."

5. Maintenance of at least a minimum normal standard of weight. Unlike anorexics, many bulimics have no emaciated figure to give them away. Of course, many women with anorexia also go on to develop bulimia (the reverse does not happen frequently). In those cases, the patients are diagnosed as having both diseases simultaneously.

THE BINGE

Do you binge? If pressed, most women would admit that, yes, they do binge from time to time—that pint of ice cream after a marital spat, the extra bran muffin after dinner, the potato chips at last week's picnic. Almost everyone eats more than they should on occasion and may consider that a binge. For someone with bulimia nervosa, however, a binge is something quite different.

Simply defined, a bulimic binge is the rapid consumption of a large quantity of food in a limited period of time, during which the patient feels out of control. The content, pattern, and duration of binges differ with every person. Some people eat anything they can find, while others pick at small portions of many different foods to hide their tracks. Some people gobble down food straight from the package or the freezer; others fix themselves elaborate meals, then prepare more food as they eat what's already done. For one woman, a binge may last an hour, for another, it may go on for several days. The calories consumed may range from fewer than 1000 to as many as 20,000. Because there's so much variability, an eating episode is probably best defined as a binge if it meets two criteria:

1. The bulimic feels that she can't control her eating.

2. She believes the amount of food is excessive, even if it's less than an outside observer might expect.

"At the height of my bulimia, my binges occupied my mind from the moment I woke up to the moment I went to bed," says Sandy, whom you met in Chapter One. "I was either thinking about what I was going to eat during my next binge, or how much I had to spend, or what else besides vomiting I could do to keep the weight off. Or I worried about preventing the next binge; I'd start out making all sorts of plans to keep myself from bingeing, only to wind up doing it anyway. After the binges I'd think about how and where I could throw up, how long it would take, and if I could fit in any exercise or perhaps take a few laxatives to help myself along, since I was going to be in the bathroom anyway. The binges became the central feature of my existence."

During a binge, someone may consume up to 7 pounds of food at a time and then vomit—and repeat this pattern 4 times a day. One woman admitted to vomiting 42 times a week—that's an average of 6 times a day. Another said she vomited as often as 15 times daily, and others report doing this as many as 18 times in a day. In fact, some scientists have theorized that some bulimics become addicted to the sensation of vomiting, much like someone else might become addicted to cigarettes, alcohol, or cocaine. Bulimics sometimes become so adept at vomiting that they can do it at will, needing nothing more than perhaps a glass of water to get the process started.

But remember that vomiting, while common among bulimics, is not an essential feature of the disease. Some women binge 3 or 4 times a day, then abuse laxatives—up to several hundred at a time—in an effort to keep their weight down. Others might chew the food to enjoy the flavor, then spit it out. Still others compensate for their eating with hours of exercise. And many bulimic patients develop longer-term strategies: one person might binge for a day, then fast completely for a day or two; another might binge for a day, then follow a drastic diet for several days, weeks, or even months between periods of bingeing. Some women can't eat normally at all; instead, they swing between periods of bingeing and periods of fasting. Only 21 percent of the patients in one study of bulimics said they ate 2 or more normal meals per day, while nearly 40 percent said they ate normal meals only once or several times a week. Twenty-one percent claimed they virtually never ate normally.

What Do Bingers Eat?

Binge foods vary as much as the people consuming them. For one woman, it was popcorn. For another, it was cottage cheese—six cartons at a time. One girl estimated she consumed 15,000 to 20,000 calories in a typical evening's binge. Another would spend her whole week's salary on food, leaving herself nothing for rent, gas, or other necessities. You probably won't be surprised to learn that the binge food of choice for many bulimics seems to be junk food—especially if it's sweet, soft, and ingestible in large quantities in the least amount of time. Ice cream, milk shakes, certain kinds of candy, french fries, cakes, cookies, fast-food hamburgers or pizza might all qualify. Others have admitted to eating baby food or even scraps from the garbage can. Many bulimics say they "crave" carbohydrates during a binge, but some studies suggest that when the nutrient proportions of a typical binge are analyzed, they're not really so different from those of a normal meal—it's just that there's more of everything. For example, it's even been found that vegetarian bulimics binge on vegetarian food.

Some bulimics claim to enjoy the food as they're eating it, but many others report feeling angry and disgusted with themselves soon into the binge even though they keep eating. Similarly, very few patients who vomit admit that they actually enjoy the act, but they do welcome the physical relief from all that food, and it eases their minds to know they won't get fat. As the binges gain more importance in a patient's life, she develops rituals around them, perhaps confining them to certain times of day and certain locations. Ultimately, she may isolate herself from the outside world completely, leaving her time only to go to work or attend school.

BINGE TRIGGERS

What sets off a binge? When asked, most bulimics give a fairly standard list of reasons, which fall into two main categories:

1. Emotional issues
2. Chronic dieting

Emotional Issues

Many bulimics report bingeing when they feel tense, anxious, or unhappy. Some patients say they eat when they can't sleep. Psychologists who treat bulimic women say that many times patients binge in response to repressed feelings of ineffectiveness, anger, and disappointment. Unable to express their feelings directly, they binge instead—stuff their feelings down with food, as it were. In one study, people more likely to binge scored higher than non-bingers on feelings of ineffectiveness (that is, feeling that they had little or no effect on their own lives or the lives of others), as well as the desire to be thin. Many bulimics say their urge to binge is initiated by minor slights or frustrations, rejection or confrontation, as well as anxiety or disappointment. Others say the desire to binge increases when they're upset. Still others say they feel panic before they eat, and that the binge-purge ritual relieves that panic. Some bulimics are so obsessed by the desire to be thin that they feel guilty after eating anything, even if they haven't binged. Thus, one patient admitted that her binges often ensued after she ate any of her favorite foods, even in small quantities.

In addition, many bulimics suffer concurrently from mood disturbances like anxiety and depression. Along with the substances they may use to try to remain thin, they may also abuse mood-altering chemicals like sedatives, amphetamines, cocaine, alcohol, and narcotics.

Chronic Dieting

Many people, bulimic or not, overeat in response to stress. But a growing body of evidence suggests that, for many people, the binge-purge pattern may also be a response to an intense struggle to maintain a weight lower than is right for them biologically. People who engage in this struggle are known as restrained eaters, while those who eat only according to the dictates of their bodies are known as unrestrained eaters.

Restrained vs. Unrestrained Eaters

Developed in the 1970s, this theory says that restrained eaters constantly watch their diet and exercise. In an effort to remain thin or at least thinner than they might otherwise be, restrained eaters eat less than they'd like, so they're in a constant state of hunger, maybe even semi-starvation. These circumstances set up the restrained eater to binge whenever confronted by stress, frustration, anxiety—anything that causes her to lose the tight control over her eating that she otherwise tries to maintain.

Unrestrained eaters, on the other hand, are those fortunate souls who eat exactly what they want, when they want. Either their shapes naturally meet the standards of beauty society has set, or these people simply do not feel so compelled to meet those standards. According to the theory, unrestrained eaters don't try to maintain the tight grip on their food intake that restrained eaters do, so they don't experience the same chronic, if subliminal hunger. Thus an unrestrained eater should not react to stress by increasing her food intake or bingeing.

Much experimental evidence confirms the notion that a person's behavior can be predicted in some situations, depending on the type of eater she is. In one typical experiment, subjects were first given questionnaires about their eating habits, and divided into groups of restrained or unrestrained eaters. Each person was then given one, two, or no milk shakes, on the pretext that the experimenters were studying the effect of the milk shakes on subsequent taste perception. The subjects were then asked to sample ice cream. The researchers predicted that after consuming the milk shakes, the restrained eaters would reason that they'd blown their diets and thus eat more ice cream, figuring they might as well enjoy the treat. The unrestrained eaters, on the other hand, would eat less following the milk shakes because they'd be full. These predictions were fulfilled, and other experiments have yielded similar results.

On the strength of such research, many experts now believe that the eating behavior typical of bulimia nervosa is, in fact, a result of chronic, restricted eating—that is, a result of chronic semi-starvation. Thus it's possible that bulimia might develop in someone who's perfectly normal emotionally, but whose prolonged dieting may instill in her the need to binge. It's been found that people who develop bulimia had been dieting for about one and a half years. Bulimics who are overweight are most likely programmed by genetics to be heavier than average, and would probably be even heavier than they are if they didn't exercise strict control over what they ate. It's also possible that they binge more on fattening foods than do thinner bulimics.

Binge Biology

If you've never embarked on a binge yourself (or even if you have), you might be wondering, "How can anyone eat that much?" The fact is, some bulimic patients say they feel hungrier than normal or can't control their appetite; others claim they crave certain foods in huge quantities. Still others say they can't tell when they're full, and that this condition existed before they developed bulimia. Perhaps people who restrict their eating develop larger-than-average appetites or higher-than-average thresholds to feeling full. In an experiment comparing satiety (satisfaction after a meal) in women with bulimia to that of non-bulimics, the bulimic patients reported lower levels of satiety five minutes after everyone had eaten a similar meal. In another study, bulimics had lower levels of a hormone called cholecystokinin, or CCK, in their blood after a meal than did non-bulimic subjects. Normally, the small intestine releases CCK following a meal. CCK stimulates contractions of the gallbladder, which, in turn, causes the pancreas to release digestive juices. When CCK is administered experimentally to animals or humans, they stop eating, leading scientists to believe that CCK may somehow help in the transmission of satiety signals from the digestive tract to the brain. Thus the finding that CCK is lower in bulimics after a meal may indicate that the physiological mechanisms telling them they've had enough are somehow impaired. But this research is still in its preliminary stages, so it's still impossible to draw any firm conclusions. Plus, the question remains: Even if such an impairment exists, did it happen before the bulimia developed, or as a consequence of the disorder or of perpetual dieting?

The Bottom Line: Why Binge?

People who treat eating disorders still vary in the degree to which they attribute bulimia to underlying emotional problems or to the problems associated with chronic dieting. The true answer will probably incorporate both theories, but it does seem clear that chronic dieting is not a realistic solution to the problem of trying to be forever thin.

The Vicious Cycle

One of the dangers of bingeing is that it may become one of the sources of the unpleasant feelings the bulimic is trying to escape, setting up a vicious cycle. A woman may binge initially because of anger or disappointment over some other event, then feel angry and guilty because of the binge. She may then spend a lot of time and energy trying to avoid the next binge, or trying to ignore the hunger or emotions that make her want to binge—many bulimics write lists of tasks or little inspirational notes to themselves, perform rituals, or keep journals with resolutions, all in an effort to stave off the next binge. Others might avoid social functions if they know food will be available, or neglect to put money into their wallet so even if they're tempted they won't be able to buy anything. Still others take long, circuitous walks to avoid seeing food shops, or even drive into the country where no stores are to be found. One desperate patient applied local anesthetic to her gums and tried to pass a wire through them, in a crude attempt to wire her jaws shut! Still another cut her fingertips so they'd be too sore to stick down her throat to induce vomiting. As you might imagine, such effort and pain only intensify whatever anxiety is weakening the bulimic's resolve in the first place, so ultimately she succumbs and the process begins again.

After the Binge

Someone might be tempted to binge once in response to negative feelings, but chances are she wouldn't make a habit of bingeing if she didn't derive some sort of benefit, no matter how unusual that benefit might appear to an outside observer. A few patients with bulimia nervosa claim to feel more relaxed during a binge, and calmer, sedated, or "high" afterward. For some, there's also a feeling of being special or unique; Sandy, for example, felt a kinship with the colorful (if unhappy) actors and writers who drank. When vomiting is part of the ritual, patients feel fresher, cleansed, and back in control of their lives.

But for many more bulimics, their feelings after the binge simply add to the self-hatred or despair that drove them to this habit in the first place. Patients report feeling guilty, worried, too full, or even still hungry, following a binge. After an entire binge-purge cycle, some bulimics report dizziness, headaches, and stomach cramps. The fact is, when practiced long enough, bingeing and purging take a serious toll on a patient's health.

PHYSICAL SYMPTOMS OF BULIMIA

While you read this section, remember that all of these symptoms don't occur in everyone who has bulimia nervosa. A lot depends on the frequency of the binge-purge episodes, the nature of the purging (vomiting or abuse of laxatives and diuretics), and the duration of the eating disorder. But it is important to bear in mind that bulimia does carry with it some serious health risks that may persist long after you've come to terms with the eating disorder.

1. Dental problems. The human stomach secretes hydrochloric acid to help with digestion. The stomach lining is specially constructed to withstand contact with this acid, which is neutralized when combined with food. But when persistently exposed to parts of the body it was never meant to contact, such as the mouth and teeth, hydrochloric acid can be extremely corrosive. Years of vomiting up stomach contents may cause severe gum disease, erosion of tooth enamel, cavities, and even permanent tooth loss. Sandy, you may recall, always covered her mouth when she smiled because she was so embarrassed by her corroded teeth.

2. Sore throat. A result of stomach acid contacting the tissues of the throat.

3. Swollen salivary glands. Frequent vomiting may also cause swelling or infection of the parotid, or salivary, glands, located near the ears, giving the cheeks a puffy appearance. The most serious cases require surgery for complete resolution.

4. Muscle weakness and cardiac malfunction. Persistent diuretic abuse, as well as vomiting, may cause dehydration and electrolyte imbalance. Electrolytes are minerals, such as potassium, that play an important role in the function of muscles and nerves. Thus in severe cases electrolyte imbalance may lead to muscle weakness, muscle spasms, and irregular heartbeat, known as cardiac arrhythmia, which may cause sudden death in rare instances. Epileptic seizures have also been known to occur.

5. Kidney damage. This is another consequence of dehydration and electrolyte imbalance. One patient had renal failure and needed a kidney transplant.

6. Tearing and bleeding of the esophagus (throat). This is a rare consequence of bingeing and purging, but it has been reported in some patients with bulimia nervosa.

7. Hiatal hernia. The pressure created by frequent vomiting may create this form of hernia, in which the stomach pushes up through the diaphragm, leading to a sensation of choking. Again, this is a rare occurrence in bulimia, but the risk is real.

8. Ulcers and calluses on the fingers and hand. In order to vomit, a bulimic will often shove one or more fingers down her throat. Done often enough, this practice may result in calluses on the hand if the hand is scratched by her teeth, or if it comes into contact with the stomach acid that comes up.

9. Consequences of laxative abuse. As mentioned in Chapter Two, these include colicky, abdominal pain, anal soreness, and in serious cases, fecal incontinence (inability to control bowel movements). On the other hand, prolonged laxative abuse may lead to dependence: the patient may be unable to move her bowels without using the laxative.

Other Characteristics of Bulimia

As you've read above, bulimics may become so obsessed with their binges and minimizing the consequences of those binges, that they may ultimately neglect most other aspects of their lives. When 275 patients with bulimia were questioned recently, 272 admitted that their disease interfered significantly with other areas of their lives. Many patients indicated social and family problems, financial woes (often because of the high cost of their food), and problems at work. Therapists have long known that people with bulimia sometimes steal food, or money to buy food, from family or friends. Shoplifting is also common, not just of food but of other items as well. In general, experts believe that bulimic patients are more impulsive than average, and place a high value on instant gratification.

WHO DEVELOPS BULIMIA NERVOSA?

As with anorexia, if you love someone with bulimia it's hard not to wonder, "Is it my fault? Have I contributed in some way? Should I be doing something different?" If you have bulimia yourself, you may be thinking, "That's it. I'm crazy. There's something wrong with me." But the fact is, bulimia nervosa is the culmination of many factors—some social, others related to your own upbringing or personality. Studies of bulimic patients in therapy have helped doctors identify some traits in families and individuals that may place some people at higher-than-average risk of developing this disease, but it's important to remember that bulimia nervosa is no one's "fault." Sometimes it's the only way someone can find to cope with turmoil and stress. Still, identifying these characteristics may help doctors identify and aid people at risk before the eating disorder sets in.

Family Characteristics

• A history of obesity in one or both parents. The experience of watching a parent struggle with a weight problem may leave a future patient with a dread of ever becoming that way herself.

• A caring, even overinvolved mother and distant father. Some psychologists who specialize in the treatment of bulimia claim that this is a persistent theme among the patients that they see: the future patient was often quite close, maybe too close, to her mother, while yearning for a closer relationship with her father. Frequently the mothers gave up careers of their own for marriage and family life, then grew disappointed and depressed. Some of these women may have projected their dreams onto their daughters, while in other cases they may have encouraged their sons to pursue interesting careers while trying to keep their daughters tied to them as long as possible. What seems consistent, though, according to these therapists, is that the father was relatively uninvolved in the daughter's life, especially after she entered puberty. It should be emphasized that some researchers question this theory, saying that the therapists who developed it may be seeing only one segment of the bulimic patient population.

• A chaotic family background. Other experts suggest that bulimics may come from a relatively chaotic family background. Substance abuse by one or both parents, physical or emotional abuse, or frequent changes of jobs and moving around, might all decrease the stability of a family unit.

Patient Characteristics

Among the traits characterizing people more likely to develop bulimia are:

• Misinterpretation of internal states or emotions as hunger. Many patients claim they can't tell when they're hungry or full; others may misinterpret feelings such as anxiety, anger, or excitement for hunger.

• Fears of emotional and biological maturity. Here, the bulimic patient may be similar to the anorexic, who also seems to fear maturity and independence. However, many bulimics maintain good jobs and social lives until relatively late in their disease, and they frequently have had sexual experience, if not ongoing relationships.

• A turbulent emotional life. Stealing, substance abuse, and a desire for instant gratification all may reflect the chaotic inner life of a bulimic, so perhaps it's not surprising that her eating habits become chaotic as well.

• A personal history of obesity and/or frequent dieting. You've seen that chronic dieting may be a cause of bingeing. Adding to that is the fact that many bulimic patients were obese prior to the onset of their illness. Someone who's suffered the indignities that obese people must endure may have an especially high stake in becoming and remaining thin, whatever the physical and emotional cost. In fact, some patients date their bulimic behavior from the time they struggled to lose weight, then became tired of starving or dieting, and so turned to bingeing and purging.

• Preoccupation with all facets of appearance. Many bulimics compete with other women in the arena of appearance. "If I wasn't the best-looking woman in the room, my evening would be ruined," one woman says. "I spent all my time worrying about how I looked, and working out and watching my food. My life is so much fuller now, because I've stopped worrying about that and can focus on other things."

• Wide swings in body weight. This is another feature of constant dieting. Some patients report weight fluctuations of 25 pounds or more within the space of just a few months.

• Involvement in a career in which body image is crucial to success: ballet or some other form of dance, acting, modeling, athletics.

Anorexia Nervosa vs. Bulimia Nervosa

As you might imagine, people who develop anorexia or bulimia have some features in common, but there are also some important differences. In general, the anorexic patient is:

• less likely to have achieved at least a minimal level of independence or personal identity.

• usually younger, still dependent upon, and enmeshed with, her family.

A bulimic patient, on the other hand, is:

• more likely to function well socially and at work, at least in the earlier stages of her disorder.

• able to maintain a relatively normal weight and may even be able to eat normally between binge-purge episodes.

• less likely to encounter life-threatening consequences as a result of her disease.

TREATMENT CHALLENGES

One positive feature of bulimia is that this disease is a little easier to treat than anorexia. Bulimics tend to be older, more independent, and may have good support systems if they haven't isolated themselves too much. They don't like having the disorder and are more willing to accept help.

We'll discuss the treatment of eating disorders in detail in Chapter Five, but you should know that bulimia does present some special challenges. Shame underscores the doubts and low self-esteem many bulimics feel, and some patients may be so embarrassed by their behavior that even if they seek therapy, they may hide the secret from the therapist. Thus, therapy may continue for several years without really doing the patient any good. Therefore, it's imperative that the bulimic find a therapist whom she trusts and feels comfortable with.

Perhaps the biggest challenge in conquering bulimia is overcoming the years of maladaptive eating habits developed from continuous dieting, bingeing, and purging. Remember, relatively few bulimic patients eat normal meals on a regular basis. Many also believe in myths regarding food, dieting, and weight that must be dispelled during the recovery process. Perhaps the worst of these myths—held by patients and some therapists as well—is that you can continue to diet, and perhaps even occasionally to binge and purge, while trying to recover. Good therapy will get the bulimic to understand the destructive role that frequent dieting has played in the development of her eating disorder; what's more, it will encourage her to come to terms with her natural body weight. This is another big challenge; most patients have unrealistic goals for their optimal weight, and therapists usually encounter a lot of resistance on this point.

For a bulimic who sincerely wants to change but finds it impossible on her own, hospitalization is recommended. There, nurses and dieticians can monitor her food intake around the clock, and make sure she doesn't vomit or purge calories in any other way. Another advantage to hospitalization: Even when the bulimic stops bingeing, her cravings for certain foods may persist for several months. In addition, she may have forgotten how to eat normally. In the hospital, her meals and snacks can be strictly controlled, taking any decision out of her own hands for a while, until her cravings subside and she learns how to eat normally again.

Group vs. Individual Therapy

Usually, bulimics participate in both group and individual therapy. Experts differ in their opinion as to which is more effective, but in general group therapy seems to help people with less severe cases of bulimia, while people with more severe cases seem to benefit more from individual sessions.

Drug Therapy

Drugs seem to have had more success in treating bulimia than anorexia, but they should never be used as a substitute for psychotherapy. Medication may be particularly helpful if the patient has a concurrent disorder like depression.

CONCLUSION

There are a couple of important points to remember about bulimia nervosa:

1. It's far more common than anorexia nervosa. If you think you're bulimic, don't let embarrassment or shame isolate you from those who can help. Good therapists, or even true friends, won't be disgusted—they'll be concerned and will try to help you overcome the eating disorder.

2. Vomiting is not an essential part of bulimia. Don't be lulled into thinking that even though you binge you're not really bulimic because you don't vomit afterward. As you've seen, overuse of laxatives or diuretics, and/or compulsive exercising, may all be forms of purging calories. Any of these is sufficient for a diagnosis of bulimia nervosa.

What's most tragic about this disease is the insight it gives into the pressure so many women feel to look a certain way. In their desire to be thin, many women make their eating habits and weight the central focus of their lives, ignoring accomplishments marking them as intelligent, productive, creative, unique individuals. Does this say more about a woman's "willpower" and propensity for self-indulgence, or about the messages she receives about her worth?

In Part II of this book, you'll learn more about putting this issue into perspective and building your self-esteem.

CHAPTER FOUR

COMPULSIVE EATING

Is compulsive eating an eating disorder?

Some experts say no, that it does not have the crippling, sometimes even life-threatening consequences of anorexia and bulimia, and that the entire concept is too subjective to permit doctors to develop diagnostic criteria like those established for other eating disorders. Some experts are also troubled by the fact that many people think of compulsive eating as an addictive disorder, similar to alcoholism or drug addiction—only the patient is addicted to food. In fact, such categorization reveals a failure to understand the true nature of addiction, and only confuses attempts to define and understand eating problems.

But others say yes, compulsive eating is an eating disorder because it represents an abnormal and counterproductive relationship with food, which is, after all, the basic definition of an eating disorder. Compulsive eaters might be said to have one of the "nonspecific" eating disorders mentioned in Chapter One, because they don't meet the official diagnostic criteria for anorexia or bulimia, but nevertheless do have a disturbed relationship with food. This book, therefore, wouldn't be complete without a short chapter on compulsive eating.

WHAT IS COMPULSIVE EATING?

Compulsive eaters eat when they're not hungry. They eat when they're happy, they eat when they're sad, they eat when they're angry, lonely, tired, depressed, excited, cheerful, or in the thrall of just about any other feeling you can name. If you're a compulsive eater, you probably feel compelled to eat in response to any strong emotion, and in that sense the eating is either out of your control, or within your control only at great cost. Any time you experience strong feelings, even positive ones, if you're a compulsive eater, you'll eat.

Some therapists believe that the payoff for compulsive eating is that it distracts the eater's mind from her real problems. Much like people with bulimia, many compulsive eaters eat, then hate themselves for it afterward. This causes the self-perpetuating cycle of more stress, leading to more eating, leading to more stress, and so on, so that the patient focuses her mind and energy on ways to keep from eating, and not on the issues that created her stress in the first place. For example, Margie's marriage was in trouble, but whenever she thought about the true source of her stress—her husband's lack of emotional support, his workaholic hours—she experienced an urge to eat. She'd then try to reason with herself not to eat. Almost invariably, she'd give in to the urge, then spend a few hours scolding herself and promising to start dieting immediately. All this preoccupation with eating and weight helped Margie forget about her dissatisfaction with her husband. In this sense, eating can be viewed as a coping mechanism for some people, because it helps them cope with their problems, albeit in a counterproductive way.

THE ROLE OF BINGEING

Bingeing, alas, is a far more common practice than you might realize. You don't have to be bulimic to binge; recent surveys have shown that many college-age women *and men* binge. The severity of the binge seems to reflect the bingers' degree of negative self-image and preoccupation with dieting. Among women, recent major life changes, like a new job or a divorce, also seem related to the severity of the binge.

It's important to remember, though, that not all compulsive eaters binge. Some just eat more, or more frequently. Perhaps you've gotten into the habit of walking to the refrigerator whenever you come home from school or work, whether you're hungry or not. Other people may eat bigger meals, taking several large helpings of each course, again regardless of whether they're still hungry. And many people develop the habit of having a snack before or after a stressful event, unaware that they're eating not from hunger, but stress. One woman, for example, realized that she always nibbled on candy when talking to her mother.

Predictors of Binge Severity

Binge eating has been documented among people of all weights, so this activity is apparently independent of weight. What's more, don't automatically assume that an obese person got that way because she binges. In fact, the results of studies in non-bulimics who binge echo those of bulimics: The tendency to binge appears to be closely related to the tendency to diet. Some studies suggest that bingers have more rigid, extreme attitudes about dieting than do people who may be obese but don't binge. In a recent survey of college girls who admitted to bingeing, the factors that best predicted the severity of the binges were:

- heightened preoccupation with food
- excessive concern about dieting
- fear of losing control over eating
- dissatisfaction with body image
- poor self-image or self-esteem
- increased stress

Once again, this raises the issue of restrained vs. unrestrained eaters: Those people who binge may be doing so as a reaction against restrained eating, while obese non-bingers may be heavy because they don't restrain their eating, and thus don't feel the need to binge.

ROLE OF SELF-ESTEEM

Among people who eat compulsively, low self-esteem seems to be a common theme. In fact, many experts believe that low self-esteem is central to the issue. If someone is overweight *and* binges, some researchers think she suffers not only from poor self-esteem, but also underdeveloped basic coping and problem-solving skills, the inability to be assertive, and deficits in managing stress and interpersonal relations. Other therapists have found that even people who don't binge, but do eat compulsively, lack self-esteem and the capacity to soothe themselves when feeling anxious or afraid. It can be said that a compulsive eater often puts herself between a rock and a hard place: She hates the way her body looks, and hates herself when she succumbs to the urge to eat. Out of this self-hatred, she punishes herself further by going on a diet, promising never to eat "forbidden" foods again—until the next time.

HOW COMPULSIVE EATING DEVELOPS

The reasons why people become compulsive eaters are actually quite simple:

• They have trouble distinguishing hunger from other feelings. Similar, perhaps, to the lack of "interoceptive awareness" that characterizes people with other eating disorders, some compulsive eaters can't tell when they're hungry and may therefore eat in response to cues that have nothing to do with their bodies' needs. For example, Margie eats dinner automatically at six o'clock every evening, even if she's just finished a late lunch at four. One man depended completely on his wife to prepare meals; when she died, he would finish entire loaves of bread or quarts of milk in one sitting, not because he wanted to, but because he didn't realize there was any other way!

Doctors believe some habits like these begin in childhood. Many parents feed a baby whenever she cries, even if she's crying because she's wet or for some other reason that has nothing to do with food. In this way, the child becomes accustomed to being fed in response to any distressing feeling or event, and this habit persists into adulthood.

• They use food to comfort themselves. There's a reason why certain foods are known as "comfort" foods: They remind us of times, most likely during childhood, when all our needs were met, we were taken care of, and the world was safe. In addition, parents often use certain foods to comfort children during times of distress—an ice cream cone after falling from a swing, perhaps, or hot chocolate in bed when the child is sick. Thus many of us reach adulthood associating some foods, and perhaps the act of eating in general, with a feeling of safety and being cared for.

• They diet chronically and experience frequent weight fluctuation. As you've seen, restrained eating often backfires, setting up the dieter for a binge. Like the bulimics who can only binge and fast, never eating normally, a chronic dieter may develop a similar problem to a lesser degree: she may diet for a while, then eat everything she wants—not a real binge, perhaps, but large portions even if she's not hungry—then diet again. In other words, many people simply haven't learned to eat in moderation.

Compulsive Eating, Dieting, and Weight

We should make it clear that a compulsive eater is not necessarily overweight. She may *think* she looks fat, but to an objective observer she may appear *perfectly* average, perhaps even thin.

Weight and body build have a strong genetic component. If neither of your parents was fat, the chances are only about 20 percent that you'll be fat. But if one parent was fat, that risk doubles to 40 percent, and if both your parents were fat, the risk doubles again to 80 percent. Thus, people who come from fat families must fight an uphill battle if they want to remain fashionably slim. In fact, many experts now believe that heavy people often don't eat more than their slimmer cousins—their biggest mistake may have been in choosing the wrong parents. Thanks to genetics, a fat person's body stores excess calories, while a thin person's body might simply burn them off through an increase in metabolic rate.

What's more, the habit of dieting to lose weight, then gaining it back, then dieting again, gaining again, and so on, may only make it more difficult to maintain a slender shape. Research on both humans and animals has shown that it gets easier and easier to gain weight after a diet; in other words, the weight comes back faster following each successive regimen because of metabolic changes that occur each time you diet. Not only that, but the proportion of fat in the weight gained increases every time. Even if you gain back only as much as you lost, more of that weight will consist of fat than it did before.

Today virtually every expert in the field of weight, obesity, and eating disorder research believes that food intake is only one of many factors determining a person's weight. It also seems clear that chronic weight fluctuation does take a toll on the body, and ultimately makes it more difficult to stay slim.

TREATMENT CHALLENGES

If you're seeking help for compulsive eating, you have several options. Cognitive behavioral therapy, discussed in the next chapter, may help because it requires you to focus on your behavior and the reasons for it. Sometimes all you need is to change habits that have become ingrained over the years, like the man who ate the whole loaf of bread because his wife wasn't there to put it away. Other people may benefit from self-help or support groups, in which members help each other in their struggle against a common problem. And for others, the solution may come in removing the source of stress that was making them eat to begin with. One woman found herself eating more and more as her job became increasingly difficult. After finding a new job that she liked, she discovered that she'd lost weight, and realized she had stopped snacking between meals without even thinking about it.

If you really are a compulsive eater, your biggest challenge may be to accept your body the way it is. If you're thin but think you're too fat, the challenge may be for you to see that your weight is, in fact, within normal limits. Once this is accomplished, therapy can then focus on building your self-esteem and determining why you feel it is critical that you look a certain way.

For someone who is naturally overweight, the challenges increase. Not only must this person grow to like herself the way she is, she must also develop the inner fortitude to fight the admonishments of a society that still largely equates obesity with laziness, ugliness, and incompetence. This is a tall order, even for the securest among us. Fortunately, the prejudice against fat people seems to be slowly diminishing, as you'll see in Chapter Seven.

CONCLUSION

Compulsive eaters come in all shapes and sizes and eat for all sorts of reasons. Some binge, others don't. One feature they all seem to share is an underlying lack of self-esteem; many also have histories of chronic dieting and weight fluctuations. To an outside observer, this eating disorder may not seem as serious as anorexia or bulimia, but if you're a compulsive eater, or know someone who is, you know that the issues involved are just as troubling and painful as those driving the skinniest anorexic or the most intractable bulimic. Part II of this book discusses the help that is available for all of these patients.

PART II:
FINDING HELP

CHAPTER FIVE

TREATING ANOREXIA AND BULIMIA

THE INTERVENTION

Sarah and Rick were terrified. For months they'd been watching their 15-year-old daughter, Katie, eat less and less. For the past few weeks it seemed as though the girl was eating nothing at all—at meals she'd just sit there and push the food around on her plate. When Sarah pleaded with her to eat, Katie would say, "I'm not hungry," or "I did eat some of it, and now I'm full." Sarah and Rick looked on helplessly as Katie's frame grew thinner and her clothes, looser.

The last straw came late one night, around 2:00 A.M. Unable to sleep, Sarah was about to go downstairs to watch television, but as she crossed the hall she heard some odd thumping sounds coming from Katie's room. She knocked, but there was no answer and the thumping continued. Alarmed, Sarah opened the door and found Katie in her underwear, doing jumping jacks. She'd been so engrossed in her exercise, she hadn't heard her mother knock.

A chill ran down Sarah's back as she saw just how skeletal her daughter had become. She resolved to do something about it the next day.

As it turned out, the confrontation was actually several days later. Rick prevailed upon Sarah to wait a few days so they could plan exactly what they'd say and present their case calmly. They knew from previous experience that Katie had answers to all their doubts, answers that sounded reasonable at the time, but fell apart when you thought about them later. What's more, as Katie's condition persisted, they'd done some reading about anorexia nervosa, and had even learned that a nearby hospital was running a highly regarded eating disorders program. They knew the longer they hesitated, the worse Katie's illness would become.

Nevertheless, now that the moment had arrived, Sarah and Rick were terrified. "What if we're wrong?" they asked each other. "What if we're overreacting? After all, most teenagers go through phases of dieting. What if there's some other explanation?" But then Sarah remembered the image of Katie's emaciated figure from the other night, and she knew her daughter had to be helped.

Rick went to get Katie. Sarah smiled nervously as they entered the living room. In as calm a voice as she could muster, Sarah said, "Sit down, dear. Your father and I would like to talk to you." Rick sat down beside Sarah, and she began.

"Honey, I'm very concerned about you. When I found you exercising the other night and saw how thin you'd become, it made me frightened. I love you, and I want to help you because I think you're doing yourself harm."

"Katie, I love you too, and I'm also afraid," said Rick. "It worries me when you sit at the table and don't eat, or when you stay in your room and don't go anywhere with your friends anymore. Your mother and I have done some reading on the subject, and we're afraid of what might happen if you keep on this way."

At this, Katie stood up and screamed, "Am I allowed to speak, or do I just listen to the two of you all night? What do you do, sit and count every mouthful I take? Do you monitor every time I come and go? For your information, I eat plenty. There's nothing wrong with me—it's the two of you who are screwed up!"

Sarah and Rick were shocked by this flood of emotions and words. They'd expected some resistance, but not like this. Nevertheless, Sarah took a deep breath and pressed on. "Honey, I can't accept it when you say there's nothing wrong. Doing jumping jacks at two o'clock in the morning isn't normal. Having nothing to eat all day except three carrots isn't normal. Your father and I are really worried about this, Katie, and we can't allow it to continue. I know it's scary to think about changing, but it's something we have to face."

Things didn't change overnight, but eventually, despite vociferous protests, Katie agreed to enter a treatment program, and Rick and Sarah participated with her in family therapy.

The confrontation with Katie is known as an intervention, because her parents saw her engaging in self-destructive activity and intervened to help her. Intervention is often used by loved ones concerned about someone's behavior, be it an eating disorder, drug or alcohol abuse, or other types of destructive acts. If you're worried about someone, intervention can be an effective means of conveying your concern, setting some ground rules and, ideally, getting her to go for help. If you'd like to try an intervention, keep these points in mind:

1. If possible, discuss your intentions with a counselor, clergyman, or family physician. Get his or her advice on the best way to proceed. You may even want this person to be present at the intervention.

2. Plan the intervention carefully. Who should be there— both parents, one parent, parents and siblings, a special close friend, the boyfriend or spouse? In general, the people who are closest to the patient, who see her most frequently, and whose own lives have been affected by her behavior are the best ones to participate. Also plan the time so there are no other distractions, and think about what you're going to say—maybe even rehearse beforehand. Remember, Rick and Sarah took a few days to decide what they were going to say, and when to say it.

3. Know your facts. Rick and Sarah used concrete examples of Katie's behavior—the 2:00 A.M. jumping jacks, her refusal to eat—to give her reasons for their concern. Two related points:

> **3A.** Don't accuse or criticize. To say "You're destroying this family," is hurtful and destructive. Just saying "You're killing yourself," sounds excessive and melodramatic, even if it might be true. You could however say that you are concerned with her health, perhaps even her life.

> **3B.** Keep the focus on yourself. Statements such as, "you're not the daughter we had a year ago," sound accusatory and put the patient on the defensive. Again, remember Rick and Sarah's example: they kept saying, "I [or we] feel this way when you do such and such," allowing Katie to see the impact of her behavior on them without feeling criticized or judged.

4. Stand firm. When Katie said, "There's nothing wrong with me," her mother replied, "I can't accept that." You may not see a miracle overnight, but that's no reason to change your position that a problem exists.

5. Expect resistance, especially from an anorexic. A bulimic may be more willing to consider what you have to say, but denial—refusing to believe that there's a problem—is one of the hallmarks of anorexia nervosa. Anorexics gain a sense of pride and identity from being thin, and feel threatened when someone tries to change that.

6. Arm yourself with the facts. Read up on the subject of eating disorders (the end of this book contains a list of places to contact for more information). Find out if there are any programs or support groups in your community. If you tell someone she needs help, know where she can go to get that help.

7. Remember the purpose of the intervention. Your goal is to get help for the person with the eating disorder. If that doesn't happen the first time, keep trying—don't give up or lose sight of your goal. Remember, the longer an eating disorder goes untreated, the worse it gets.

8. Acknowledge the patient's fears. Sarah did this when she commented that change could be scary. For an anorexic or bulimic, the thought of changing habits she's had for months, perhaps years, *is* scary. An anorexic may also fear that you're just trying to make her fat. Don't belittle these concerns, even if they seem irrational to you. Reassure her that you want to restore her health, not make her fat, even though she may not be able to realize that right now. And again, stand firm.

9. Don't wait. The longer you delay, the more entrenched an eating disorder becomes. It's especially important to intervene early because the chances are it won't work immediately. It may take several days or weeks for an anorexic to agree finally to get help—and she may never agree, you may have to take her in under duress. A bulimic, on the other hand, may agree more readily.

10. Don't forget your own needs. An eating disorder takes a toll on family life. Go for counseling, find a support group, do whatever you need to do to make sure you're taking care of yourself properly.

What Now?

Essentially, the goals of eating disorder therapy are similar for anorexia and bulimia, but the circumstances may differ, depending on the disease. As noted before, the chances are that someone with anorexia won't seek help on her own— she'll arrive, probably unwillingly, with one or both parents. And because she's most likely still living at home, family therapy will probably be part of her treatment. This doesn't mean that if you're the parent of an anorexic you've failed in some way—it simply means that the family members need new ways of communicating with each other so they can change the environment that fostered the development of the disease.

Bulimics, on the other hand, usually are older and may have already been living independently for some time. Often they have good jobs and may even have already started families of their own. Someone with bulimia generally knows she has a problem, and may long for help but may be too embarrassed to confess her secret to anyone. For these women, group therapy is important so they can start learning that many, many other people suffer from the same disease. If it's your own eating habits that are troubling you, rest assured that the professionals at eating disorder clinics have seen and heard it all. Behavior that may seem shameful to you merely tells them that you're hurting and want help.

Finding a Program

Now that you've decided to find help for yourself or someone you love, where do you start? Your family physician or pediatrician is a good beginning. Doctors are more knowledgeable about eating disorders today than even as recently as twenty years ago, and most now realize that they are challenging illnesses that need specialized treatment. If you have a family physician, or better yet a pediatrician, he or she is probably familiar with the best treatment programs in your area.

If that's not an option, many hospitals now have programs for treating eating disorders, ranging from complete inpatient therapy to outpatient groups. If there's a hospital near you, you might simply call its department of psychiatry or community outreach and ask if they have such a program. Even if they don't, they may be able to refer you to one that does. University medical schools, and the hospitals affiliated with them, are also good sources. Again, ask for the department of psychiatry. Should all else fail, some of the organizations listed in Chapter Eight maintain nationwide lists of programs and therapists for referral.

When considering a program, here are some questions to ask:

• What are the credentials of the staff? Of the person or people in charge of the program?

• What is the experience of the staff? How long has this program been in existence? What is the success rate?

• What are the components of this program? How long is the assessment process, and what does it consist of? How long does the inpatient component last, and what does it consist of? Is medication ever prescribed? If so, under what circumstances, and what kinds? How long is the follow-up period?

• Will my insurance pay for any or all of this treatment? Not all policies cover this kind of therapy. Check with your insurance carrier, insurance agent, or the person in your company who handles these matters.

Remember, a close and trusting relationship between patient and therapist is an essential part of the therapeutic relationship. The patient must feel comfortable with the people treating her—or at least with her primary therapist—or there's a good chance the therapy won't be as effective as it could be. In the words of one expert, "Don't believe anyone who tells you they've discovered a cure for eating disorders, or that theirs is the only way that works. Above all, follow your instincts. If something doesn't feel right to you, keep looking."

THE TREATMENT PROCESS

Goals of Treatment

The success of therapy for eating disorders depends upon many factors: the patient's own personality and desire to change; the duration of her eating disorder; the age at which the disease began; her family background; her level of social and vocational skills; and the concurrence of other disorders such as depression, to name a few.

It's important to remember that there's no "cure" for eating disorders. You can't give someone a pill, or say a magic word, and watch the disorder disappear. These illnesses concern issues that most patients have struggled with, and will continue to struggle with, for most of their lives. But a good treatment program will help bolster self-esteem and teach participants how to cope with their problems without resorting to self-destructive behavior. For patients who need it, the program will also help restore physical health and strength. In general, then, the three major goals of eating disorder therapy are:

1. Reversing dangerous or life-threatening physical symptoms.

2. Teaching the patient how to eat normally again and enjoy a more relaxed relationship with food.

3. Probing, with the hope of changing, her destructive thought patterns regarding eating, weight, and food.

If you could take a survey of the leading eating disorder programs, you'd find that the most successful ones have two essential components: therapists with whom patients develop trusting, supportive therapeutic relationships, and an approach that addresses both the patient's fears about weight and its effects on her self-esteem, and the underlying psychological issues that helped the disease flourish.

ASSESSMENT

Before someone enters treatment, inpatient or outpatient, her general physical and mental state, the severity of her eating disorder, the existence of any concurrent disorders, and her willingness to change must be assessed.

For eating disorder therapy to work, the doctors and therapists involved need as much information as possible about the people they're trying to help. If you're the parent of an anorexic, they may want to meet you, too, but the focus will be on her, at least until you assemble for family therapy. An eating disorder involves every facet of someone's life: her image of herself, her relationship with family and friends, and her ability to assert herself and make her needs known. As we've noted, most people with eating disorders derive a large portion of their identities from the eating disorder— that is, through it they can see themselves as thin, or special, or strong. Imagine how it must feel to develop a trait of which you're especially proud, only to be told you've got to change it! That's the task facing the person who enters treatment for an eating disorder—only in this case, the trait of which she's so proud is destructive to her. But that's why the assessment must be as detailed as possible: so the counselors can tailor the therapy to each patient individually, thereby increasing her chances of recovery.

Questionnaires

Several specialized questionnaires have been developed to assess patients with eating disorders. They help evaluate someone's attitudes toward weight and shape, and clarify psychological features like personality traits, degree of social functioning, and similar issues. Two questionnaires in wide use are the Eating Attitude Test (EAT) and the Eating Disorder Inventory (EDI). EAT consists of 26 questions designed to measure the presence of disturbed eating patterns and determine if the patient has anorexia nervosa. With 91 questions, EDI (technically, EDI-2, because a new, revised edition is now in use) is more ambitious, designed to measure a range of psychological symptoms thought to contribute to the development and maintenance of eating disorders: drive for thinness, body dissatisfaction, perfectionism, interoceptive awareness (awareness of inner body states such as hunger or fatigue), social insecurity, asceticism (self-denial of pleasure or indulgence), bulimia, ineffectiveness, interpersonal distrust, fears of maturity, and impulse regulation. In addition to initial assessment, therapists often use EDI to gain a better understanding of the patient, plan more effective treatment, and measure her progress.

It's important to realize that, by themselves, these questionnaires cannot be used to diagnose eating disorders. That can only be done in an interview, where a doctor can observe the potential patient face-to-face. What EAT and EDI *can* do is indicate who is most likely to have an eating disorder, and what some of her unique issues might be.

The Interview

The assessment interview helps the doctor or therapist obtain a clearer picture of the patient's life-style, her current weight, history of dieting and weight fluctuations, eating habits, and attitudes toward weight and shape. Attendance at work or school, relationships with family, spouse, lover, or friends, and outside interests and occupations are all of interest, because they shed light on her coping skills, degree of independence, and the extent of her isolation. Needless to say, you should also expect the doctor to be curious about past and current attempts at dieting, bingeing, and vomiting; use of laxatives, diuretics, and diet pills; moods during meals and binges; patterns of food intake; and feelings about being the "right" weight and shape. Finally, the interviewer will want to know, is this person ready to change? Will she be open to receiving therapy? Even the best therapy can fail if the patient herself is not committed to it.

A physical assessment is also important. If someone is obviously emaciated and unable to think clearly, or highly agitated with an irregular pulse and other signs of possible electrolyte imbalance, she may be a candidate for immediate hospitalization, whether she wants it or not. And as you learned in Chapters Two and Three, such extreme physical deterioration is bound to affect her mental functioning and ability to benefit from therapy.

TREATMENT OPTIONS

Following the evaluation, you'll receive recommendations for treatment. Don't be alarmed if the proposed treatment course isn't exactly like those you may have read about in articles or books, or heard about from friends. There's no standardized method for treating eating disorders. According to one prominent authority, "The best treatment is the one that works." What's most important is that the program be comprehensive, combining psychotherapy with nutritional therapy and counseling and, if necessary, specialized medical attention. Drug therapy, employed in some cases, is discussed in Chapter Six.

Individual Psychotherapy

Perhaps the most important aspect of psychotherapy for eating disorders is the development of a warm, trusting relationship between the patient and her therapist. People with eating disorders frequently find it difficult to trust others, especially when required to discuss eating habits they themselves find bizarre and disgusting—they're afraid everyone else will be disgusted too. Remember also that one of the strongest components of an eating disorder is an irrational fear of becoming fat. It takes a high degree of trust for a patient to believe a therapist when he or she says, "This food won't make you fat," so she can relinquish her fears and start developing more normal eating habits.

Traditional Psychotherapy

Traditional methods of psychotherapy encourage a patient to ponder her childhood, dreams, and unexpressed feelings for insight into her current behavior. By recognizing the role of these subliminal influences, the theory goes, the patient will gain insight into her actions and change them.

In the treatment of eating disorders, this type of therapy is probably best used as an adjunct to other methods. Psychologists now know that learning about the roots of your behavior won't necessarily get you to change that behavior, and eating disorder treatment can't really be considered successful unless the patient's eating behavior changes. In fact, as we've mentioned, many patients spend years in traditional psychotherapy without ever revealing that they have an eating disorder! Thus, by therapy's end, they may know themselves a little better, but they still have their disorder. On the other hand, as the patient gets her eating under control, traditional psychotherapy may help her recognize and handle some of the feelings that contributed to the disorder.

Behavior Modification

This form of therapy is perhaps the complete opposite of traditional psychotherapy, because it ignores underlying feelings completely and concentrates only on changing behavior. Behavior modification operates on a very simple principle: Reinforce a desired behavior through rewards; punish or ignore an undesired behavior. For example, an anorexic patient who meets a predetermined weight goal might be permitted to see a movie or take a day off from school. If she fails to meet that goal, she might not be allowed to watch television. A similar system of rewards and punishments would be worked out with a bulimia patient.

As you might have guessed, this form of therapy works best when the patient is in the hospital, where the staff can control incentives like TV, field trips, etc. And indeed when first tried, behavior modification did appear to work, if only temporarily. Unfortunately, clinicians later discovered that the overall effect was counterproductive. Patients found the hospital stay so unpleasant that they performed the desired behaviors just enough to have themselves declared recovered and discharged. Once out, they promptly returned to their old ways.

Cognitive Behavioral Therapy

Cognitive behavioral therapy, sometimes called CBT or CB, combines the best aspects of traditional psychotherapy and behavior modification. This method requires awareness *(cognition)* and challenge of self-destructive behaviors and thoughts, followed by appropriate changes in *behavior*. Thus the patient works on the inner motivations and the outer manifestations simultaneously.

CBT involves the following steps:

• Heightening the patient's awareness of her own thought patterns.

• Teaching her to recognize the connection between certain feelings, self-destructive thoughts, and unhealthful eating behavior.

• Examining the validity of certain thoughts or beliefs.

• Substituting erroneous beliefs with more appropriate ideas.

• Gradually changing the fundamental assumptions that underlie the development of eating disorders.

All of us probably subscribe to "erroneous beliefs" at one time or another; the difference is that for a woman with an eating disorder, they're more extreme, more deeply entrenched, and influence her entire approach to life. Some thought patterns typical of such a belief system:

Black and white thinking. You can also call this "all-or-nothing" thinking: the belief that, if everything isn't perfect, disaster is just around the corner. For example, a bulimic patient might believe, "I ate a piece of candy today. I've blown it completely, so I might as well binge." In CBT, she would be encouraged to examine that reasoning. What does she mean by "blown it"? Has she ever seen a thin person eat one or two pieces of candy, and no more? Now that she's eaten the candy, has she instantly gained all that weight she's trying to avoid? If she ate only one piece of candy, doesn't that indicate that not every treat has to lead to a binge? Such questions are designed to get the patient to reexamine her thinking, and admit the possibility that perhaps there's another way of viewing the situation.

Errors of attribution. "I knew it," Linda said when she arrived for her latest therapy session. "I gained two pounds this morning—all because I had that blueberry muffin last week. You see what I mean? I can't eat that stuff!" Linda made a mistake in assessing cause and effect: she thought the blueberry muffin was the cause of the unwanted effect —the weight gain. In fact, after a little probing by her therapist, she acknowledged that her menstrual period, which always caused her to retain a few pounds of water, was due in a few days.

Magical thinking. Linda's statement also contains an example of this type of erroneous belief: "I can't eat that stuff!" The smallest indulgence in a "forbidden" food means instant obesity. Someone else might believe "My body can't tolerate carbohydrates. It turns them into fat instantly," or "I'm addicted to sugar. One taste of something sweet and I'm out of control." Such ideas ascribe unrealistic, almost magical properties to food and the human body that really don't exist. Here a therapist might use nutrition books or even ask the program's nutrition expert to sit in and explain how the body metabolizes food, to help the patient understand that there's really no such thing as a "bad" food.

Personalization. Anne, a 15-year-old anorexic, spent the summer in an eating disorder program, and had gained about seven pounds when she returned to school in the fall. Her math teacher from the previous year, who had noticed Anne's extreme thinness at the time, saw her in the hall and said, "Anne! You look great! Did you have a good summer?" For the rest of the day, Anne worried. "Have I gotten so fat that people notice it? Did she know I was in therapy? No one was supposed to know that. Did I really look that bad last year?" And so on. Anne had taken the teacher's innocent remark far too personally, a reflection perhaps of the low self-esteem that characterizes eating disorders. In therapy, she learned how to take such remarks more at their face value—the teacher was glad to see Anne, hadn't known she was in therapy, but just thought she looked good.

Magnification. Anne's reaction to her teacher's remark also contains an example of magnification—the tendency to exaggerate things. The teacher's compliment turned into a comment that she'd gotten fat. Earlier in treatment, Anne told her therapist, "Did you know what that dietician wanted me to eat today? A sandwich *and* a banana! I've already gained a pound—I'm turning into a disgusting, fat pig."

Often, faulty thought patterns develop similarly to faulty eating patterns—they begin as perhaps harmless aberrations that eventually become so much a part of your life, you can't imagine existing without them. In therapy, you can learn to recognize when you start falling into such patterns and can stop yourself and say, "Wait a minute. Am I overreacting? Is there another way I can look at this?"

CBT has been practiced with good results on people with bulimia and has been recommended for the treatment of anorexia, but its long-term effect on the latter is still not known for sure. Anorexics often need longer-term treatment than CBT is designed to provide; bulimics generally respond in about four months. Studies are now under way to measure the outcome of anorexics treated with CBT.

GROUP THERAPY

For people who have never tried it, the idea of therapy can be frightening. Baring your innermost thoughts, confronting your darkest fears—it's a scary prospect. And the thought of doing all this in a group may make it even worse! In fact, however, the purpose of group therapy is just the opposite: It's meant to provide a supportive network of people who know what you're going through, and want to help you build your self-confidence so you no longer have to be ruled by your doubts and fears.

Group therapy seems to be especially valuable in the treatment of bulimia. According to one recent survey, group therapy was more cost-effective than drugs or individual therapy (although individual therapy had a greater immediate effect). Because many bulimics believe they're the only ones who engage in such horrible practices, it's often therapeutic—not to mention a tremendous relief—to learn that other people do these things too. Therapy groups ask for a firm commitment; some even have patients sign contracts requiring them to attend a certain number of sessions, maintain a normal weight, and follow regular eating patterns. Some groups may last only a few weeks, while others go on for a year or more. Some researchers have suggested that people with less severe cases of bulimia tend to do well in groups, while more severe cases respond better to individual therapy. Most experts, however, believe that ideal therapy consists of both.

Less is known about group therapy for anorexia nervosa. Some therapists worry that far from trying to change their behavior, anorexics in a group might compete to see who can maintain the lowest weight or go the longest without eating. And again, the protracted therapy many anorexics need make many groups unsuitable, since it's unusual for one therapy group to last that long.

FAMILY THERAPY

Many experts recommend family therapy as part of the treatment for anorexia nervosa, because anorexics are frequently younger than bulimics and still living with their families. If you're the parent of an anorexic, you may wonder why the whole family has to go into therapy. Are they implying that you're crazy? Or that you've failed as a parent? Of course not. Family therapy simply allows the therapist to observe the dysfunctional patterns that helped give rise to the eating disorder. During family therapy, the therapist can watch how family members communicate with each other; even the places the different members occupy in the therapist's office reveal a great deal about family alliances and interactions. Some therapists even try to watch the family at meals together, to pick up clues about familial attitudes toward mealtimes, eating, and food. All of this can ultimately help the anorexic patient recognize unhealthful family patterns and become more assertive, and the family as a whole may learn better ways to help each member get his or her needs met.

Features of Family Therapy

As the name implies, this type of therapy treats the whole family as the patient. Similar to an anorexic's individual therapy, there's first an initial assessment phase, during which the therapist gets acquainted with the other family members. In this initial phase, the therapist will also help family members develop a plan for helping the person with the eating disorder: for example, how to help her start gaining weight, or stop bingeing and purging. These problems have to be attended to first, because her health is in the balance.

Once the eating disorder is more or less under control, family therapy can move into the next phase. Now the therapist can help the family look at the eating disorder in the context of the family's function as a unit. For example, it may come out that the disorder began just as the parents began contemplating a divorce, or when the mother became pregnant again. If the patient has come to believe that she can't express her doubts and fears openly, or if for some reason she starts to feel ignored or unloved, she may have taken it out on herself by convincing herself that she was too fat. Expressing these feelings is uncomfortable for everyone involved; in therapy you'll learn that conflict and disagreement are a normal part of family life. The therapist can show you that feelings can be verbalized and conflicts resolved without threatening the entire family structure. Ideally, in this phase the parents will learn how to help their daughter grow, and the daughter will learn how to become more independent.

Most good therapists aim toward giving their patients the skills to function well without using therapy as a crutch for the rest of their lives. Family therapy is no different: in the last phase, the therapist will ultimately try to wean the family off therapy. He or she may recommend other forms of therapy, such as marital therapy for the parents, if necessary, or individual therapy for a particular member, but the ultimate goal is to encourage the healthy, independent functioning of each member and the family unit as a whole.

Family Therapy for Bulimics

This section has emphasized therapy for the families of anorexics, but families with a bulimic member can also benefit. The phases of therapy are similar. In addition, some experts have recommended some dos and don'ts for bulimic families (although they would probably work just as well for anorexic families).

Do:

• let family members choose what they eat

• hold the patient responsible for her chores (if kitchen chores are too stressful, she can choose other household chores—but she has to do them)

• hold her responsible for her behavior; for example, she has to pay for the food she eats during a binge, or clean up the bathroom following a purge.

Don't:

• make remarks about her weight or appearance

• hang on every bite she eats, or excessively watch over her in other areas

• fight during meals

• assume you know what she thinks about something. Even if you're right, it's better to ask and let her express her opinions herself.

NUTRITIONAL THERAPY

The goal of nutritional therapy is to help the patient realize that she can eat anything she wants, in moderation. To accomplish that, she must be freed from her dread that anything she eats will cause her to gain weight. For the anorexic, this involves breaking through her wall of denial—her insistence that she likes the way she looks, she likes the way she is, there's nothing wrong with her, her eating habits are fine. No subtle psychological tricks are involved here; instead, a recalcitrant patient must be confronted with gentle but firm proof that she's too thin—loss of menses, the fact that she feels cold all the time, that it's too painful for her to sit in a hard chair, or simply that she's 30 percent below ideal weight for her age and height—followed with sympathetic but persistent cajoling to eat. This simple approach, acknowledging the patient's fears but insisting that she eat anyway, has had surprisingly good results.

For the bulimic, the challenge is to learn that eating small amounts of her favorite foods does not inevitably lead to a session of binge and purge. Some therapists believe that until a bulimic has learned to eat normally again, decisions regarding what and when to eat should be made by someone else, with the patient simply eating everything she's given despite any misgivings she may have. Many therapists encourage bulimic patients to view the food as "medicine" that will protect them against future urges to binge. Toward that end, it's been recommended that the patient's weekly meal plan incorporate small amounts of previously "forbidden" foods (that is, foods associated with bingeing), so she can learn that consuming these items does not automatically lead to a binge. If the desire to binge does become overwhelming, some doctors recommend three strategies: distraction, delay, or parroting.

• Distraction. Here the patient simply distracts herself from thoughts of bingeing or food with another activity—going for a walk, talking on the telephone, watching television, listening to music, reading, any harmless activity that takes her mind off food. Earlier in this book, we noted that many bulimics already engage in some of these activities to keep from bingeing, but this just creates a vicious cycle of more tension, increased urge to binge, etc. The difference here is that these steps are now being performed in a therapeutic context, under the guidance of a physician or counselor, and in conjunction with other forms of treatment.

• Delay. Before she binges, the patient delays it with some enjoyable task such as reading a favorite poem or listening to music. This tactic is meant to break the connection between the *desire* to binge and the *act* of bingeing. It may also serve as a distraction that helps the desire wane.

• Parroting. Just as a parrot repeats what it hears, the patient is encouraged to repeat several phrases to herself until they're firmly anchored in her system of beliefs. "I can eat normally, I don't need to binge," and "Eating is part of getting better, this food is my medication," are two examples of phrases that patients might use.

Self-Monitoring

Recording their eating patterns, as well as the thoughts and feelings that accompany meals or urges to binge and purge, helps patients identify the negative feelings and counterproductive thinking that contributed to their disorders. Some programs have a patient monitor her feelings just prior to a binge; others ask her to record details about her food intake during the binge to explore attitudes about weight, shape, or eating that may underlie some of her practices. Studies have shown that bulimics who keep a diary experience a 25 to 30 percent decline in symptoms.

Further Education

Many therapists encourage their patients to learn more about their eating disorders. Armed with knowledge about the development and course of eating disorders, their effects on the thought processes, and the faulty thinking that maintains them, a patient is even better equipped to conquer the beliefs and myths that made her sick in the first place.

WHO NEEDS A HOSPITAL?

Outpatient therapy for eating disorders is often successful, but there are some instances in which the patient must stay in the hospital, if only for a brief period. These include:

• Serious or life-threatening physical deterioration. One of the goals of hospitalization is to prevent the patient from harming herself any further while she receives therapy.

• The inability to end the binge-purge cycle. Some bulimic patients truly want to change, but can do so only under the constant supervision of hospital staff.

• The presence of concurrent disorders such as drug abuse, alcohol abuse, or panic disorder. These issues must be addressed as soon as possible before the eating disorder can be truly resolved.

Programs vary somewhat between hospitals, but a typical session includes these elements:

• A two-week assessment and diagnostic phase prior to admission

• An inpatient phase lasting an average of six weeks, consisting of:

    nutritional counseling and therapy for weight gain
    medical evaluation
    daily individual therapy
    daily group therapy
    family therapy (if appropriate)

• Follow-up lasting up to one year, consisting of individual, group, and family therapy, according to the patient's needs.

SELF-HELP AND SUPPORT GROUPS

Many self-help and support groups exist for people who will not or cannot enter formal treatment programs, or whose formal therapy is finished but want some additional help. The groups vary widely in quality and philosophy, depending on the expertise of the people leading them (if any), and the self-awareness of the members. At their best, the groups provide guidance, emotional support, suggestions for more help, and a social outlet for people who might otherwise be very isolated. The group reminds the patient that she's not the only one who does what she does, that others have engaged in the same behavior and recovered. In this way, she learns that she's not hopeless. A good group can help a patient weather and grow through a crisis, as well as cope with the slings and arrows of everyday living, without resorting to her old behavior. In groups run by therapists, the therapist's role will change as the group members become stronger and more adept at assuming responsibility.

One drawback that's been associated with less formal groups is that, unlike therapy groups, they do not require regular attendance, so there may be a certain amount of turnover or instability in group membership, which may trouble some people.

DIFFERENCES BETWEEN SELF-HELP AND SUPPORT GROUPS

Although the terms are often used interchangeably, self-help and support groups are actually slightly different. Self-help usually refers to those groups that consist entirely of people suffering from eating disorders; no professionals are involved (unless they happen to have an eating disorder as well, in which case they would attend the group as a member, and not in a professional capacity). In a self-help group, members are encouraged to discuss their personal histories, current circumstances, how things used to be for them, and how they are today. Familiar with the dysfunctional thought patterns of someone with an eating disorder, group members can point out faulty ideas and challenge them in a way that seems less judgmental than when coming from a family member or professional therapist.

Support groups involve the help of one or more professionals, although their roles may change as the needs of the people in the group change. While not engaged in formal group therapy, the therapists can ask questions and guide discussions in ways that might not occur to a person not trained in these matters.

OVEREATERS ANONYMOUS

Because it is so far-flung and so popular, Overeaters Anonymous (OA) deserves a brief look.

Founded in 1960, OA is a granddaughter of the 12-step programs whose prototype is Alcoholics Anonymous (AA). The philosophy underlying OA is that compulsive eating is a progressive disease, like alcoholism or drug addiction, and that it can be controlled by following the same 12 steps followed by alcoholics. The first step is to admit that one is powerless over food; the second step is to admit that a Higher Power (referred to by many members simply as HP) can restore the member to "sanity," and the third step involves turning one's will and life over to God. The remaining steps require the member to confront and atone for her mistakes, to lead a more spiritual life, and to carry the message of OA to others. OA is free to anyone who wants to join, although voluntary contributions are requested at each meeting. Anorexics, bulimics, and compulsive eaters are welcomed by OA; the only requirement for membership is, according to the organization's literature, "a desire to stop eating compulsively."

Virtually every expert interviewed for this book had mixed feelings about OA. One authority stated flatly that "to recommend that an anorexic attend OA amounts to malpractice." The last thing an anorexic needs is to hear that her eating is out of control and she must look to God or a higher power for more control! If anything, she must learn that food is a source of nourishment and pleasure, and that a little self-indulgence is good once in a while.

Another problem seems to be in the concept of overeating as an addiction or progressive disease like alcoholism. It is not. The biggest difference is that you *have* to eat, but you can exist very nicely without ever touching alcohol or drugs. For people already struggling with issues about eating, encouraging them to view food as a potential enemy over which they must exert control is a risky business indeed.

Finally, OA is a self-help group. There is no professional guidance, and leadership changes each week, on the theory that this prevents one member from attaining more responsibility or prestige than anyone else. What this means is that people suffering from various degrees of psychopathology must rely on each other for help and support. It also means that someone in desperate need of professional help may attend meetings for months or even years without making any real improvement, because the people around her aren't trained to recognize her needs.

Now for the good news: Despite the drawbacks, millions of people would feel lost without the OA meetings they attend. Lots of crying and hugging occurs in these meetings; for many people, it's the only place where they feel completely safe to express their fears, frustrations, and doubts. For people raised in families where feelings were never discussed, OA can be a safe haven. Its philosophy probably works best for bulimics, who can become very isolated and who may indeed feel as though they've become addicted to their binge-purge behavior. Indeed, the word "binge" was first applied to alcoholics who would go off on drinking bouts lasting several days or more. If you find OA helpful, by all means continue to go. Just remember that no one program or philosophy is perfect, and if at any time you feel it's not for you, it's not a personal failure to drop out. Also remember that someone with a full-blown, firmly entrenched eating disorder will probably need more help than OA alone can give her.

CONCLUSION

By reading this book, by considering treatment for yourself or a loved one, you've taken the first and most important step toward recovery: You've acknowledged that there's a problem. That takes a lot of courage.

It's tempting to follow that statement with, "It's all downhill from here," but of course that would be false. What *is* true, however, is that through effective intervention and treatment, you can help loosen the destructive grip an eating disorder places on the patient and those around her. A good treatment program won't offer an overnight cure, but it does offer hope.

CHAPTER SIX

DRUGS USED IN THE TREATMENT OF EATING DISORDERS

Doctors have experimented with a wide array of drugs to help treat eating disorders, with varying degrees of success. Many types of medication have been said to help anorexics gain weight and maintain it, but a lack of well-designed studies prevents experts from making firm conclusions. Better results have been achieved in the treatment of bulimia, for which at least one new drug (fluoxetine hydrochloride, or Prozac) seems to hold promise in helping to prevent binges. Nevertheless, many questions remain, and most people who treat eating disorders believe that drugs should never be the first choice of treatment, but should follow nutritional support and psychotherapy. Doctors may sometimes prescribe one or more of these drugs if they feel the patient is not responding quickly or completely enough to psychotherapy, but remember that drug treatment is only *one* part of a comprehensive treatment plan. If you or a loved one encounters someone who claims to treat eating disorders with drugs alone, run! Virtually all experts agree that drugs should *never* be used as the sole treatment for an eating disorder.

Before receiving any drug, patients should undergo a complete physical examination, including tests of liver, heart, and kidney function. *Do not use any of these products if there's even the slightest chance that you are pregnant.*

What follows is a rundown of the drugs most likely to be used in treating anorexia and bulimia. In addition to remaining alert for side effects, the manufacturers of these compounds recommend that patients tell their doctors about any other medical conditions they may have and what other medications they're taking. It's also important for patients to advise their doctors of any drug-related allergies they might have.

Tricyclic Antidepressants (TCAs). As their name implies, these compounds were used originally in the treatment of depression, and that remains their primary use. However, these drugs have also been used in the treatment of anorexia and bulimia. They're called "tricyclic" because of their three-ringed chemical structure.

Scientists still aren't sure exactly how TCAs exert their effect. However, it's generally agreed that these drugs somehow influence the activity of chemicals known as neurotransmitters, used by nerve cells to help relay messages through the brain. Patients may not experience therapeutic effects for several weeks, but side effects, such as drowsiness, dry mouth, constipation, and low blood pressure, may occur immediately. Other side effects may include confusion, blurred vision, and dizziness, as well as increased appetite for carbohydrates or sweets, which may be especially troubling to someone battling an eating disorder.

Examples of TCAs include amitriptyline (Elavil), imipramine (Tofranil), and nortriptyline (Pamelor).

Monoamine Oxidase Inhibitors (MAOIs). These medications get their collective name from the fact that they inhibit the action of an enzyme called monoamine oxidase, which breaks down neurotransmitters in the brain when their action is finished. When this enzyme's action is inhibited, brain neurotransmitters remain high and are thought to help relieve the symptoms of depression and eating disorders. The MAOIs currently in use are isocarboxazid (Marplan), phenelzine (Nardil), and tranylcypromine (Parnate).

Like the TCAs, these compounds are used in the treatment of both anorexia and bulimia nervosa. Their main drawback is that they may seriously intensify the effect of other drugs, including methyldopa (Aldomet, used to treat high blood pressure), levodopa (Dopar, Larodopa, prescribed for Parkinson's disease), and amphetamines, which are often abused by patients with bulimia. Intracranial hemorrhage sometimes occurs when amphetamines and MAOIs are taken simultaneously. This is also a danger when MAOIs are taken with over-the-counter cold or allergy pills containing the chemicals ephedrine or phenylpropanolamine (PPA). PPA is also found in over-the-counter diet pills. Clearly, a physician must know exactly which drugs a patient uses before he prescribes MAOIs.

Patients who take MAOIs should avoid foods containing the amino acid tyramine, since this may interact with the drugs and lead to a dangerous rise in blood pressure. The foods to be avoided include:

Cheeses and dairy products
American, processed*
Blue
Boursault

* 1991 by Facts and Comparisons. Used with permission. Table from page 1194 of *Drug Facts and Comparisons,* 45th ed., 1991. St. Louis: Facts and Comparisons, a Division of the J.B. Lippincott Company.

Brick, natural
Brie
Camembert
Cheddar
Emmentaler
Gruyère
Mozzarella
Parmesan
Romano
Roquefort
Sour cream
Stilton
Yogurt

Meat/Fish

Beef or chicken liver
Meats prepared with tenderizer
Fermented sausages (bologna, pepperoni, salami, summer
   sausage)
Game meat
Caviar
Dried fish (salted herring)
Pickled herring
Shrimp paste

Fruits/Vegetables

Avocados (especially if overripe)
Yeast extracts (Marmite, etc.)
Bananas
Figs, canned or overripe
Raisins
Soy sauce
Miso soup
Bean curd

Alcoholic Beverages

Beer and ale (imports, including some nonalcoholic)
Red wine (especially Chianti)
Sherry

Foods Containing Chemicals that Raise Blood Pressure
Anything with caffeine
Anything with chocolate
Fava beans (overripe)
Ginseng

Trazodone. Also called Desyrel, trazodone is another antidepressant that has been shown to decrease the frequency
of binge-purge episodes in bulimic women, without the significant side effects of TCAs or MAOIs (trazodone is in a
different category of compounds). It also seems to help
these patients stay in remission for up to 19 months.

Nevertheless, despite its low incidence of side effects in
the treatment of eating disorders, the possibility of side effects does exist. Skin conditions and disorders of the digestive tract and liver are only a few of the effects reported in
people who have received trazodone for depression, although it should be emphasized that these reactions are
relatively uncommon. More common, and much less serious, side effects include constipation, loss of sexual drive,
and water retention (edema).

Lithium carbonate. This drug's mechanism of action in
treating eating disorders remains unknown, but it has been
shown to induce weight gain, reduce the frequency of bulimic episodes, and enhance mood. Among the most common side effects, nausea can be diminished by taking lithium after meals or in a timed-release form; itchiness and
rash may be alleviated by using the drug in the liquid,
rather than solid (pill) preparation. These side effects have
not been well documented in anorexics; in bulimic patients,
they can be minimized by making sure blood levels of lithium remain within certain strict limits. Lithium toxicity is a
risk for patients who binge, purge, abuse sodium-depleting
diuretics, and reduce their intake of liquids. Signs of lithium

toxicity include diarrhea, vomiting, nausea, drowsiness, weak muscles, and loss of coordination, followed by giddiness, vertigo, ringing in the ears, and seizures if the toxicity is not treated.

Lithium carbonate has several trade names, such as Eskalith, Lithane, or simply Lithium Carbonate.

Fluoxetine Hydrochloride. Better known as Prozac, this medication has lately been the focus of much controversy. Doctors initially thought of this drug as an effective, relatively safe treatment for depression, and then discovered that it could also be used to help bulimics resist the urge to binge. Recently, however, it's been reported that some people taking Prozac have considered and even attempted suicide. The Food and Drug Administration (FDA) investigated these claims and concluded in 1991 that there was no credible evidence that Prozac causes suicide. Most doctors believe that when prescribed in the right dose and under close supervision, Prozac is safe.

Some of the side effects associated with Prozac include skin rashes and impairment of kidney and liver function. The rashes usually remit as soon as the drug is discontinued, although some patients have needed steroids or antihistamine to clear their skin completely. Kidney and liver problems are rare but can be serious, so people who have renal or hepatic disease should use this drug less often or in lower doses, if at all.

Chlorpromazine. This compound is generally used in the treatment of psychotic disorders such as schizophrenia, or for children with severe behavioral problems. It's been tried in anorexic patients, but most experts question its value for this purpose. What's more, chlorpromazine may have serious side effects, most notably tardive dyskinesia, a disorder characterized by jerky, involuntary movements of the limbs and face. Other side effects, such as liver and kidney problems, are more rare but can be serious when they occur. Chlorpromazine is made by several companies and is known by its generic name.

Metoclopramide. Metoclopramide stimulates movement of the digestive tract, and has been reported to help anorexics gain weight and tolerate food. It's also used to combat the nauseating effects of cancer chemotherapy, so it's possible that this compound may somehow make it less easy to vomit after a binge. Side effects of metoclopramide, which may also be known as Reglan, Clopra, Maxolon, Octamide, or Reclomide, include drowsiness, dizziness, and exhaustion.

Properly used in the context of a comprehensive program, some medications can help lift patients out of depression and mitigate the desire to binge and purge. Thus, under some circumstances, there is a role for drug therapy in the treatment of eating disorders. The key is that they be prescribed by a doctor familiar not only with the drugs themselves, but with their specific use in people with anorexia or bulimia.

CHAPTER SEVEN

MORE HELP

SUGGESTIONS FOR FAMILY AND FRIENDS

Eating disorders affect an entire family. It's agonizing to watch someone you love starve herself or make herself sick while resisting your best efforts to help. On the other hand, it's impossible to pretend that nothing's wrong—this is one situation where you can't "act as if." When a child develops a problem around something as basic as food, many parents ask themselves, "Is it my fault? Did I do something wrong? Did I put too much pressure on my child or have unreasonable expectations? Was I a bad parent?" It's important to remember that eating disorders have many causes. While it cannot be denied that the presence of an eating disorder often (but not always) does point to a more basic problem in family dynamics, it also cannot be denied that the child also goes to school, the movies, perhaps a ballet class, and so on. She's influenced by the prevailing culture as much as by her upbringing. Alone, no one person, not even a parent, has enough power to induce someone to develop an eating disorder.

If you've been living with someone with an eating disorder, chances are you've already tried to help her. Maybe you're reading this book in the hope of finding a different approach, having seen that little is accomplished through nagging, scolding, begging, pleading, bargaining, or manipulating. The fact is, eating disorders only rarely get resolved without professional help—the vast majority of sufferers must enter specialized programs if they really wish to recover. Don't blame yourself for lacking skills only a trained professional could be expected to have.

If you believe that someone you love has an eating disorder, level with her. Don't keep silent in the hope that it's just a phase—the longer the disease persists, the sicker the patient gets and the more difficult it is to treat her. Refer back to Chapter Five for information on conducting an intervention. If the idea of trying a full-fledged intervention right off the bat seems too intimidating, maybe you'd like to try a less extreme alternative first to see what kind of response you get. And there is always the chance that the person with the eating disorder is silently begging for help, secretly hoping that someone will notice her predicament and help her find a way out. She may be relieved to have someone else break the ice. Here are a few tips for confronting someone with an eating disorder, without necessarily engaging in a real intervention:

Collect yourself before you begin. Try not to become emotional. Express your concern, but in as calm and nonjudgmental a way as possible.

Expect resistance. This is why you must remain calm and collected. While there is that chance that she'll inwardly welcome your concern, remember that most people with eating disorders are embarrassed and frightened. People with anorexia nervosa usually deny that there's anything wrong with them at all. Stand firm if the patient becomes angry or hostile or denies that she has a problem.

Remain firm in your position that she needs help, despite her denials. Make it clear that you're doing this because you're concerned for her health, maybe even her life, and not because you think she's crazy or a bad kid.

Hold her responsible for her behavior. If she makes a mess in the kitchen after a binge, it's her responsibility to clean it up. If she lacks the energy to go to school in the morning, she's still responsible for maintaining her grades. You can't force an unwilling person to go for therapy, but you *can* confont her with the consequences of her actions. What's more, establishing some firm ground rules will help restore some order and stability to *your* life.

Remain open to getting help yourself. You need not say this to the patient as you're confronting her, but in your mind remember that eating disorders do take their toll on the entire family if the patient is living at home. As you've seen, many programs require family therapy as part of the patient's treatment.

In the same vein, make sure your own needs are met. One way to remain calm in the face of the patient's anger and not feel too threatened at the thought of family therapy is to make sure that you are taking care of yourself. If you feel you need individual psychotherapy, seek it out. There are also support groups for relatives of people with eating disorders, where family members can express feelings of anger, fear, resentment—anything at all. The people at your chosen eating disorder program may be able to direct you to such a group, or you can contact one of the organizations listed in Chapter Eight.

TIPS FOR BUILDING SELF-ESTEEM

As you learned in Part I, low self-esteem is one of the common threads that stitch together the different eating disorders. Preoccupation with weight, fear of becoming fat, and placing undue importance on appearance all reflect the patient's fear that if she just "lets herself go," and shows the world who she really is, she'll be rejected instantly. One of the goals of good eating disorder therapy is to have the patient appreciate her own intrinsic worth, which has nothing to do with her appearance or the way she eats.

How easy it would be if you could rebuild your psyche by reading a few pages in a book! Unfortunately, few accomplishments are that easy. The information and tips that follow can't begin to substitute for a course of therapy, but they can reinforce whatever help you do seek. They may also serve as reminders of some of the issues dealt with, in far greater depth, in therapy.

REASONS FOR LOW SELF-ESTEEM

How does someone develop low self-esteem? There seem to be several factors at work:

Believing shape determines worth. People with eating disorders have come to believe that they are worthless and unacceptable unless they're thin, and of course they can never be thin enough to be satisfied. If they are overweight, their shame and self-loathing are even greater. That's because they believe they have nothing to offer except their appearance, which is flawed.

Reliance on external factors to determine self-worth. Instead of loving and valuing herself from within, someone with low self-esteem measures her worth through external signals. These might be a grade on an exam, a time in a race, approval from a friend, a number on a scale, or any external and often arbitrary standard of value. Margie, for example, was crushed when her best friend didn't comment on her new hairdo. "Maybe it really doesn't look good," she complained. "Maybe I look silly. I knew I shouldn't have gone to that hairdresser—he was too young. I look lousy." With more self-esteem, Margie would have enjoyed her hairdo because *she* liked it, not because of what other people said or didn't say. Besides, she had no way of knowing if her friend Betsy really liked it or not. Perhaps Betsy was preoccupied, or upset over something in her own life, or maybe she didn't even notice Margie's hair! The point is, it's dangerous to derive your self-esteem from external sources, because they're so unpredictable. Far better to rely on the inner standards you set for yourself.

Thinking of yourself as ineffective or incompetent. Feelings of ineffectiveness are one of the hallmarks of eating disorders in addition to low self-esteem. If someone feels powerless over her life or environment, it stands to reason she won't be able to develop much self-respect.

Tips for Boosting Self-Esteem

• Ask yourself: "If time and money were no object, what would I be doing right now?" Would you be a movie star? An artist? An opera singer? A cowboy? A construction worker? The sky's the limit; let your mind soar. Now find a way you can put a little of that experience into your daily life. If you've always dreamed of being a movie star, for example, take acting lessons. If you wanted to be a construction worker, perhaps you can develop a hobby restoring furniture, or maybe even houses. The point to this exercise is to find some activity that gives you pleasure and to do it for the sheer enjoyment of doing it—not for any external reward or payoff. In this way you'll start feeling good about things you do for yourself, not from compliments from friends or other external incentives.

Devote yourself to something you already do well. Developing a new skill involves patience and the risk that you don't have the aptitude for it, so be sure to spend some time also at something you *know* you're good at. Carol derives tremendous satisfaction from designing and knitting sweaters in beautiful colors; Marie gets a lift every time she comes home and sees the houseplants she's so carefully tended. Sometimes the greatest pleasure comes from a simple task, beautifully done.

• Invent an imaginary devil's advocate, or ask a friend to be one. That's what Margie could have done when her friend didn't comment on her hair. As she started thinking, "Betsy didn't mention my hair. I must look lousy," her inner advocate could have challenged her with questions like, "Do *you* like your hair? How would your life be different if Betsy paid you a compliment? What if Betsy said she hated your hair? You don't always agree with Betsy's taste anyway— you hated that dress she wore last week." In this way, someone with low self-esteem may begin to realize the essential problem of relying on outside reinforcement to feel good about herself.

• Ask yourself, "why is it so important that I look a certain way?" How would your life change if you were ten pounds thinner? Would it make you better at your job? More fun at parties? A better wife or mother? If your answer to any of these questions was yes, explore that further. If being ten pounds thinner would make you more fun at parties, why? Because you'd feel more confident and secure? More relaxed and flirtatious? More attractive? Less self-conscious? Even these answers reveal that you're tying your essential self-worth to your weight and external appearance. So ask yourself this: Would Mother Teresa be any less saintly if she weighed any more? Would Eleanor Roosevelt have accomplished more if she'd been beautiful?

• Imagine a world in which weight was permanently fixed. Whatever your weight at age 16, that was your weight for the rest of your life—there would be no possible way to change it. What would your life be like then, if weight were simply not an issue to worry about? Would you still put off buying nice clothes? Would you still work out for two hours a day, every day? Would you still have half a grapefruit for dessert, instead of the chocolate cake? This exercise is designed to get you to see the sacrifices you make and the ways you put your life on hold because you're not at a certain weight. What all of this really amounts to is self-punishment for not attaining some predetermined, and possibly arbitrary, weight goal. Perhaps you'd feel a little happier and better about yourself if you stopped putting off certain things like buying new clothes. Even if you intend to reach a lower weight some day, you still have to get dressed now. Why not look your best, no matter what your weight?

• "Act as if." This slogan, borrowed from OA and other 12-step programs, actually continues the line of reasoning begun in the paragraph above. Act as if you're thin. Act as if you're beautiful. Act as if you love yourself, warts and all. Ironically enough, people who act as if they love themselves start getting better feedback from the rest of the world, which makes it easier for them to love themselves, in fact.

• Notice the other people around you. This is most effective if you belong to a health club or gym, where people walk around the locker room in various stages of undress.

How many perfect bodies do you see? Human beings come in a wide variety of shapes and sizes, very few of them perfect. Besides, what you consider perfect may not appear that way to someone else. That girl over there who's built like a fashion model may be consulting a plastic surgeon for breast implants, because she's self-conscious about her flat chest.

If You're Overweight

Overweight people have a tough time in this society, especially if they're obese. Prejudice against fat people is persistent and deep-rooted. Even many doctors, who should know better, often admit they don't like fat people in general and fat patients in particular. If your body naturally wants to be at a higher weight than society deems acceptable, you must battle not only your own inner demons, but the outer dragons as well.

One way to start boosting your own self-esteem, and perhaps start changing the minds of those around you, is to arm yourself with a few facts about your condition:

• Weight, like height and skin color, is largely a matter of genetics. If both your parents are fat, the chances are overwhelming that you'll never look like a fashion model, no matter how much weight you lose.

• Except in extremely severe cases (100 pounds overweight or more), excess weight does not seem to be the health hazard it was once thought to be. Even among people with high blood pressure or high blood cholesterol, a loss of only 5 to 10 pounds is often enough to bring them back down into a normal range. There is no evidence that fat people take more sick days from work or visit doctors more often than do thin people.

• Food intake is only one of several factors that determine weight. Genetics is another, as mentioned above. Previous attempts at dieting may have affected your metabolism, as might your current level of activity. The image of the fat person stuffing herself is pretty much false. In fact, some evidence suggests that heavy people don't eat more than anyone else. And remember, not everyone who binges is fat.

• There is no evidence that fat people score lower on IQ tests, college entrance exams, or any other measure yet devised of competence or intelligence.

• Tests of psychological health reveal no difference between fat and thin people.

Some Other Ways to Boost Self-Esteem

• Learn to accept yourself. In preparation for this, develop a healthful nutrition and exercise plan. You may want to consult a nutritionist to learn better eating habits. Make it clear you're not looking for a reducing plan—just some guidance in eating a normal, healthful diet. The same holds for an exercise program: make it clear that you're exercising to benefit your heart, bones, and lungs, and not to attain some impossible shape. The weight you reach when practicing the healthiest possible life-style is probably your natural, genetically determined weight—the weight at which you can begin to love and accept yourself.

• Join a self-help or support group. Don't feel depressed about your weight—feel angry at a world that's too ignorant or stupid to understand you. For more insight into this, you may want to read Suzy Orbach's classic book, *Fat Is a Feminist Issue* (Berkley Books, 1978). A group consisting of other people experiencing the same thing will validate your feelings and help you see that there are other people in your corner. For more information on groups in your area, contact the National Association to Advance Fat Acceptance (NAAFA), a national advocacy group that promotes self-acceptance among fat people. NAAFA even has a Fat Admirers division for thin people who are attracted to fat people— there are plenty of Fat Admirers out there! Some chapters of OA also hold special meetings for people who are, or have ever been, overweight by 100 pounds or more. Addresses and telephone numbers for both organizations are given in the following chapter.

• If you find that your problems with self-acceptance and self-esteem resist all your attempts at improvement, consider professional help. Choose someone knowledgeable about obesity and eating disorders, so that he or she will not spend time looking for psychological reasons for your weight, if none exist.

CONCLUSION

This book has tried to give you some insight and hope about disorders that can be frightening, frustrating, and occasionally even fatal. No one's saying recovery is easy, but lots of help and support is available, because there are lots of people with eating disorders out there. No one has to struggle alone.

Many questions about eating disorders still exist. For example, why does society hold obesity in such contempt that so many people find these behaviors preferable to being fat?

What is the best way to help a child develop self-esteem or help someone rebuild self-esteem that's been damaged? Why does one person develop an eating disorder, while someone coming from exactly the same circumstances does not? These are just a few of the questions researchers are pursuing; perhaps you've come up with a few more of your own.

There are some encouraging signs. The wide media exposure given eating disorders in the last few years has made these diseases easier to detect, and the people who have them feel less reticent about coming forward and asking for help. At the same time, scientists are finally beginning to succeed in chipping away at the great stone wall of prejudice that fat people must overcome to achieve more acceptance in today's society. Progress has been slow, but it's been there. One actress, a former model, was asked to *gain* ten pounds for a recent film role in which she played a glamorous career woman. And some of the models in some recent Paris fashion shows were actually said to have cellulite! Perhaps we're heading back to a more Rubenesque ideal, or better yet, an era in which someone is ideal just the way she is.

CHAPTER EIGHT

FOR FURTHER INFORMATION

ORGANIZATIONS THAT HELP PEOPLE WITH EATING DISORDERS AND THEIR FAMILIES

Anorexia Nervosa and Associated Disorders (ANAD)
PO Box 7
Highland Park, IL 60035
(708) 831-3438

Established in 1976, ANAD offers free hot-line counseling, provides information, and maintains a nationwide list of support groups. It also urges diet companies and other businesses to change their advertising, exposes insurance discrimination, and practices other forms of consumer advocacy on behalf of people with eating disorders.

Anorexia and Related Disorders, Inc. (ANRED)
PO Box 5102
Eugene, OR 97405
(503) 344-1144

ANRED provides booklets, pamphlets, and information packets to people who request information.

Bulimia Anorexia Self-Help (BASH, Inc.)
6125 Clayton Avenue, Suite 215
St. Louis, MO 63139
Hot Line: (800) 762–3334

Originally established to help people with eating disorders, BASH now offers treatment and sponsors research on mood disorders caused by depression, phobias, and chemical imbalances. It also has its own local therapy groups, maintains a speakers bureau, and holds an annual conference. BASH publishes a magazine covering all sorts of issues, from eating disorder case histories to crack addiction to burnout in eating disorder therapists.

Center for the Study of Anorexia and Bulimia
1 West 91 Street
New York, NY 10024
(212) 595–3449

While not a referral organization, the Center will send an information packet listing national organizations.

FOR FURTHER INFORMATION

American Psychiatric Association (APA)
Division of Public Affairs
1400 K Street
Washington, DC 20005
(202) 682–6000

The APA is the national professional organization of psychiatrists.

National Association to Advance Fat Acceptance (NAAFA)
PO Box 188620
Sacramento, CA 95818
(916) 443–0303

NAAFA provides advocacy and support for fat people around the country. Its various chapters hold local social and business meetings, and the organization sponsors an annual conference.

National Institute of Mental Health (NIMH)
Eating Disorders Program
Building 10, Room 3S231
Bethesda, MD 20892
(301) 496–1891

One of the National Institutes of Health, NIMH will send a free pamphlet to callers.

Overeaters Anonymous (OA) World Service Office
Box 92870
Los Angeles, CA 90009
(213) 657–6252 (This is a 24-hour number. If you get a machine, leave a message and they will get back to you by mail or phone. Or call telephone information in your town for the number of your local chapter.)

INFORMATION ON RESEARCH STUDIES AND PROGRAMS

Behavioral Medicine Program/Health and Behavior Research Branch
Room 11C06
National Institute of Mental Health
5600 Fishers Lane
Rockville, MD 20857
(301) 443–4337

FOR MORE INFORMATION ON READING MATERIALS

Public Inquiries
Room 15C05
National Institute of Mental Health
5600 Fishers Lane
Rockville, MD 20857
(301) 443–4513

GLOSSARY OF TERMS

amenorrhea—Failure to menstruate. A woman may never have menstruated, or may have menstruated and then stopped. Amenorrhea may occur for many reasons, but it is a diagnostic symptom of anorexia nervosa, because it indicates that the patient's body weight has fallen below a minimum healthful standard.

anorexia—The Greek word for loss of appetite; also an abbreviated name for the disease anorexia nervosa.

anorexia nervosa—An eating disorder characterized by an extreme fear of becoming fat, self-starvation in an effort to avoid becoming fat, and amenorrhea.

antidepressant—A drug administered to relieve severe depression. People with eating disorders sometimes receive antidepressants, either because they suffer from depression along with the eating disorder, or because some antidepressants are thought to mitigate the symptoms of eating disorders.

asceticism—Rejection of pleasure or self-indulgence as decadent or weak-willed. Some anorexics are considered ascetic because they do not adequately fulfill their bodies' needs, and consider it a badge of honor to deny themselves food or other necessities for as long as possible.

behavior modification—A form of psychotherapy that involves reinforcement of desired behavior through reward, and extinguishing of undesired behavior through punishment.

binge—The rapid, uncontrolled consumption of a large amount of food in a short period of time.

body image—The inner self-portrait most people have in their minds. Distortion of body image was once thought to be a predisposing factor in most cases of eating disorders; now most experts believe that eating-disordered patients see themselves accurately, but don't like what they see.

bradycardia—Slow heartbeat.

bulimia—The Greek word for "ox hunger," implying a huge appetite; also an abbreviated name for the disease bulimia nervosa.

bulimia nervosa—An eating disorder characterized by alternating periods of bingeing and vomiting, laxative abuse, diuretic abuse, and/or strenuous dieting. Most bulimics also are excessively afraid of becoming fat and place an unrealistic premium on physical appearance.

CB or CBT—An abbreviation for cognitive behavioral therapy (see below).

cholecystokinin (CCK)—A hormone released by the small intestine that plays an important role in digestion, and is thought to be important in helping people feel full after a meal. Some people with bulimia nervosa have lower-than-average levels of cholecystokinin in their blood following a meal, leading to speculation that a deficiency of this hormone may play a role in developing or perpetuating the disorder.

cognitive behavioral therapy—A type of psychotherapy in which the patient recognizes faulty thought patterns and changes her behavior accordingly.

constipation—Lack of a bowel movement for at least three days.

eating attitude test (EAT)—A questionnaire administered to those who have, or are thought to have, eating disorders. The test measures the presence of disturbed eating habits and other characteristics typical of eating disorders.

eating disorder inventory (EDI)—A questionnaire administered to those who have, or is thought to have, eating disorders. The Eating Disorder Inventory measures the psychological features thought to contribute to the development and maintenance of eating disorders, and helps in patient diagnosis and treatment.

edema—Water retention in the tissues, sometimes leading to a swollen or bloated appearance. Some people with anorexia nervosa develop edema due to starvation, or when they first begin eating normally again.

electrolytes—Minerals that exist in the blood and body fluids as electrically charged particles, which are then capable of conductiong nerve and muscle impulses, assisting in chemical reactions, and many other activities essential to normal body function.

esophagus—The tube leading from the throat to the stomach; sometimes also called the gullet.

hypotension—Abnormally low blood pressure.

hypothermia—Abnormally low body temperature.

interoceptive awareness—An awareness of one's inner states or feelings, such as anger, joy, hunger, or fatigue. Some experts believe that interoceptive awareness in people with eating disorders is decreased.

lanugo—The development of abnormal, baby-fine hair all over the body, often seen as a symptom of starvation.

menses—The flow of menstrual blood.

monoamine oxidase inhibitors (MAOIs)—A class of antidepressant drugs thought to exert their effect by inhibiting the action of an enzyme in the brain called monoamine oxidase. These drugs have been used, with varying degrees of success, in the treatment of eating disorders.

osteoporosis—Loss of bone density leading to greater risk of bone fracture and the hip breaks and spinal degeneration often associated with old age. Osteoporosis is thought to have several causes, including estrogen deficiency and certain forms of malnutrition, both of which are present in anorexia nervosa.

parotid glands—Salivary glands located near the ears. In people with bulimia nervosa, the parotid glands sometimes swell or become infected, giving the patient a puffy-cheeked appearance.

restrained eaters—People who watch their weight and food intake continually to maintain their weight below what it might naturally be. Restrained eaters are thought to be more likely to binge or eat compulsively in response to factors such as stress, anger, disappointment, etc.

tricyclic antidepressants (TCAs)—A class of antidepressant drugs with a distinctive, three-ringed chemical structure. These drugs have been used, with varying degrees of success, in the treatment of eating disorders.

unrestrained eaters—People who do not worry about what they eat; they eat what they want, when they want. Unrestrained eaters are thought to be less likely to binge or eat compulsively in response to emotional factors such as stress.

INDEX

ABOUT THE AUTHOR

Norra Tannenhaus holds degrees in biopsychology and nutrition from Vassar College and Columbia University. She has written extensively on health, medicine, and nutrition for consumers and doctors, and her magazine articles have appeared in such major publications as *Self, Glamour,* and *Mademoiselle.* She is the author of *Learning to Live with Chronic IBS* and *What You Can Do About Diabetes* in the Dell Medical Library. *What You Can Do About Eating Disorders* is her sixth book. A New Yorker at heart, Norra Tannenhaus currently makes her home in Los Angeles.